HORMONES 101

A SIMPLE GUIDE TO UNDERSTAND AND ENHANCE YOUR HEALTH WITH CLARITY AND CONFIDENCE WITHOUT THE CONFUSION

ELIZA SHARPE

CONTENTS

INTRODUCTION

It started with a Monday morning that should've been ordinary. Thirty-four-year-old Eva sat at her desk, a cup of coffee in hand, as the familiar glow of her laptop screen greeted her. But something felt...off. Her heart was racing, her face was flushed, and the energy she usually relied on to kick-start her week had vanished. Instead, a wave of irritability crashed over her, unprovoked and unsettling.

By lunch, a splitting headache joined the party, accompanied by a strange, bloated heaviness she couldn't shake. She chalked it up to stress, maybe dehydration—or the looming deadline at work. But the next day, the symptoms lingered, joined by an inexplicable craving for chocolate and a sudden impatience with her coworkers.

When a sleepless night and an unexpected emotional breakdown followed later that week, Eva realized this wasn't just a bad week. Something deeper was happening. "What is wrong with me?" she whispered into the darkness, her phone lighting up with search engine queries about anxiety, fatigue, and mood swings.

What Eva didn't yet know was that she was standing on the edge of a discovery that would change her life: the intricate, delicate, and downright fascinating world of hormones. Her symptoms weren't just random; they were signals—clues from her body about shifts she couldn't yet see. And so began Eva's deep dive into understanding her hormonal health, an eye-opening journey that revealed the powerful role hormones play in every aspect of a woman's well-being.

Eva's story might feel familiar. Whether it's a rogue hot flash in your 30s, mysterious weight gain, or brain fog that sneaks up on you, hormones often send their first messages as whispers. This book is your guide to decoding those whispers, understanding the rhythm of your body, and learning how to thrive through every stage of hormonal life. Because when it comes to hormones, knowledge isn't just power—it's freedom.

Did you know that a staggering 80% of adults report experiencing confusion or frustration about their hormones at some point in their lives? That's right, you're not the only one wondering what this new mysterious symptom is and should you go to the doctor or not. A recent survey highlighted this widespread misunderstanding, revealing that many people struggle to find reliable information about their hormonal health.

So, why should you care about understanding your hormones? Well, let's put it this way: hormones are the unseen worker's of your body's engine. They influence everything from your energy levels and mood to your skin health and long-term well-being. Ignoring them is like trying to tune a high-performance engine without checking the gauges—it's bound to get rough.

This book promises to take the mystery out of hormones and provide you with clear, actionable insights. By the time you're done, you'll have a much deeper understanding of your hormonal health. You'll feel reassured and empowered to make informed decisions, whether it's about your diet, lifestyle, or those peculiar cravings.

Here's a quick peek at what's in store: We'll start with sex hormones, exploring the myths and truths about estrogen, testosterone. For instance, we'll debunk the myth that testosterone is only important for men, and we'll uncover the truth about estrogen's role in women's health. Then, we'll move on to metabolic hormones, where you'll meet insulin and its colleagues. Stress hormones won't be left out either—we'll unravel the mysteries of cortisol and adrenaline. Finally, we'll tie it all together with practical lifestyle changes to help balance these hormonal maestros. Each section builds on the last, creating a guide that's as comprehensive as it is engaging.

This book is for you—the person who wants clarity without confusion. Maybe you're tired of googling symptoms and end up more confused than when you started. Or perhaps you're simply curious about what makes your body tick. Either way, you're in the right place.

As you read this book, I encourage you to consider it both a learning experience and a practical guide. It contains easy-to-understand explanations, practical tips, and real-world applications. It's like having a friendly chat with a knowledgeable buddy who just happens to know a lot about hormones. You'll feel equipped with the knowledge and tools to take charge of your hormonal health.

So, are you ready to dive in? With an open mind and a dash of curiosity, you'll soon find yourself navigating the world of hormones with confidence. Empowerment and clarity are just a few chapters away. Let's get started!

This book focuses on 19 essential hormones—carefully chosen from the more than 50 produced by the human body—to give you a clear understanding of their functions and their profound impact on your well-being. To make this journey even easier, I've included an icon chart to add a visual of the hormones in this book.

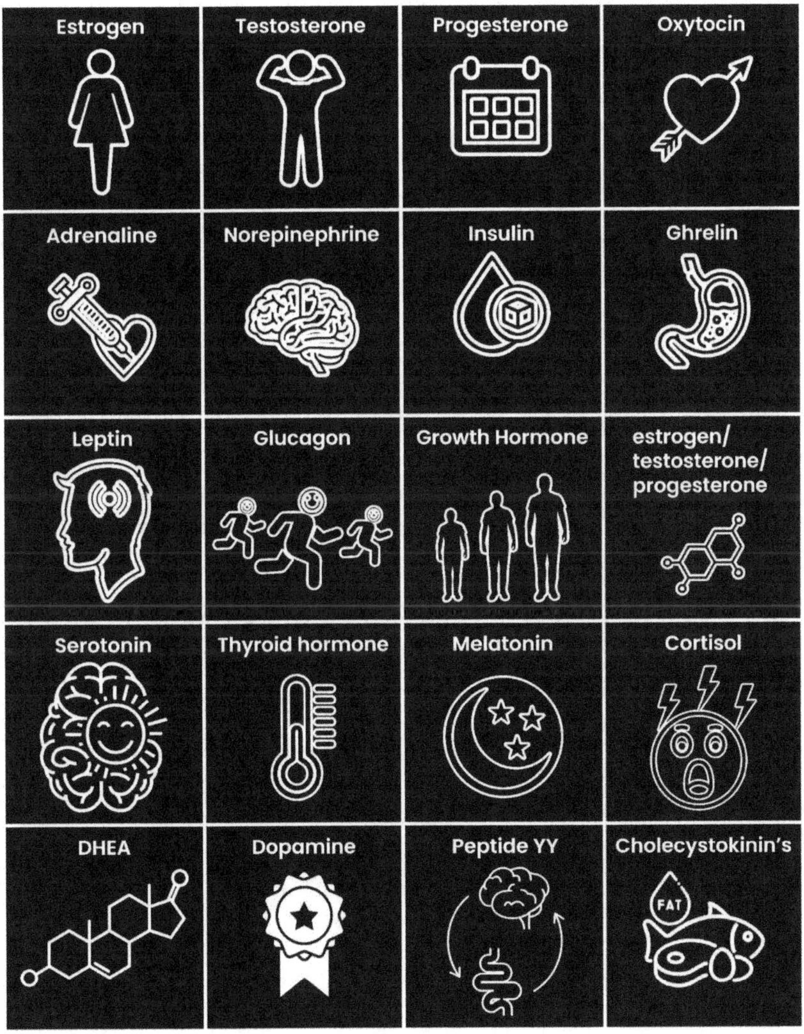

Estrogen	Testosterone	Progesterone	Oxytocin
Adrenaline	Norepinephrine	Insulin	Ghrelin
Leptin	Glucagon	Growth Hormone	estrogen/ testosterone/ progesterone
Serotonin	Thyroid hormone	Melatonin	Cortisol
DHEA	Dopamine	Peptide YY	Cholecystokinin's

CHAPTER 1
HORMONE BASICS: TINY PLAYERS, BIG IMPACT

Imagine you have a team of tiny superheroes inside you, each with a special job and a personality to match. That's kind of like what hormones are! They're these little chemical messengers zipping around in your body, telling different parts what to do—like when to sleep, how hungry to feel, or why you're suddenly super annoyed with your spouse. Think of hormones as your body's group chat, where everyone has something important to say (sometimes a little too loudly). When they're all working together, everything runs smoothly, but when one of these little guys decides to go rogue, well, that's when things can get... interesting. So, let's dive in and get to know these tiny messengers with big personalities! But what exactly are these hormones responsible for besides turning us into emotional ping-pong balls?

HORMONAL HARMONY: UNDERSTANDING THE BASICS

Let's set the stage by defining hormones. Think of them as the body's postal service, delivering vital messages from one part of the body to another. With approximately 50 different hormones at play, these chemical messengers are secreted by endocrine glands —those quiet overachievers like the thyroid, adrenal glands, and pancreas. Much like the backstage crew at a concert, these glands are crucial yet unseen, ensuring everything runs smoothly. Hormones aren't just whispering sweet nothings to your body; they're bustling around, influencing growth, mood, metabolism, and even your appetite.

Now, hormones come in various flavors. We have sex hormones, estrogen, progesterone, and testosterone, which are like the body's VIP backstage passes and are made from cholesterol. Then there are peptide hormones, the smaller, punchy ones like insulin, made from amino acids and working tirelessly to regulate blood sugar levels. Lastly, amino acid-derived hormones, which include adrenaline, are the ones that give you that sudden jolt when you see a spider or hear unexpected footsteps in the dark.

The hormonal lifecycle is a fascinating spectacle. Hormones are synthesized, often from cholesterol or amino acids, and released into the bloodstream—the body's version of express delivery. Once they've delivered their message, they're broken down and escorted out like a guest who's overstayed their welcome. This process is tightly regulated by feedback loops, a bit like a thermostat keeping your home at a comfy temperature. When hormone levels veer off course, the body sounds the alarm, adjusting production to restore balance.

But what happens when this delicate balance tips? Hormonal imbalances are sneaky little devils. They can lead to mood disorders that make you feel like you're on an emotional rollercoaster. According to a study in *Verywell Mind*, hormones like serotonin and cortisol are key players in mood regulation, and when they're out of whack, you're left wondering why you cried over a burnt toast. Physically, imbalances might cause unexplained weight changes, fatigue, or even skin issues, as if your body decided to throw a party and forgot to invite you.

Understanding the basics of your hormonal health isn't just for science enthusiasts or those with a penchant for medical dramas. It's crucial for anyone who wants to feel better, live healthier, and maybe even understand why they crave chocolate at the oddest times. This chapter is your backstage pass to the world of hormones, offering insights, clarity, and a touch of humor to guide you through the hormonal maze. So, buckle up and prepare to meet the unseen forces that run the show inside you.

YOUR BODY'S ENGINE: HOW HORMONES COMMUNICATE

Think of your body like a high-performance sports car, with each hormone as a finely tuned part that keeps you running at top speed—everything works best when all the parts are in perfect sync. How do these hormonal components hit the perfect performance tune? It starts with hormone receptors, the body's personal bouncers. These receptors sit on the outside of your cells, waiting for the right hormone to come along and bind with them—like a lock waiting for its key. Once the hormone fits into its receptor, the real magic begins. This binding triggers signal transduction pathways, which is just a fancy way of saying that a series of biochemical events gets set in motion. These pathways are responsible for everything from telling your cells to absorb sugar to signaling your muscles to grow. Think of it like flipping a light switch; the initial action is small, but the result is illuminating.

But hormones don't work in isolation. They love a good collaboration, interacting with each other to keep your body's functions in harmony. Take insulin and glucagon, for instance. They're like the yin and yang of blood sugar regulation. When insulin is busy storing sugar, glucagon waits in the wings, ready to release sugar when levels get too low. It's a classic case of synergy, where the combined effect is greater than the sum of its parts. Sometimes, though, hormones clash, like adrenaline and insulin, during stress. Adrenaline wants you to have energy to fight or flee, but insulin aims to stash that energy away. This push-and-pull keeps your body in a dynamic balance, a hormonal dance that's both intricate and essential.

The nervous system plays a crucial role in this hormonal engine, mainly through the hypothalamus-pituitary axis. Picture the hypothalamus as the master mechanic, overseeing the engine from its position in the brain. At the same time, the pituitary gland acts as the lead component, interpreting and amplifying the mechanic's signals. This axis is a major communication highway, releasing neurohormones that regulate everything from stress responses to growth. It's a delicate balancing act, one that requires constant fine-tuning to keep everything running smoothly.

However, like any sports car engine, disruptions can occur. Environmental stressors, nutritional deficiencies, and chronic stress are the unruly audience members that can throw the whole performance off-key. Environmental disruptors, like chemicals found in plastics, can mimic hormones, confusing your body's natural processes. You might think you're signaling for a calm, steady rhythm, but instead, it's a chaotic drum solo. Nutritional gaps can leave your hormone signals weak or ineffective, like trying to drive your car with no gas. And let's not forget stress. Chronic stress can flood your body with cortisol, turning your fine-tuned engine into a noise racket.

So, what can you do to keep your engine running smoothly? Be aware of these disruptors and take steps to minimize their impact. Focus on a balanced diet rich in nutrients, manage stress through mindfulness or exercise, and be cautious of products containing potential endocrine disruptors. Remember, your body is a master-piece in progress, and understanding how your hormones communicate can help keep the music playing beautifully.

THE HORMONAL BALLET: BALANCING ACT FOR OPTIMAL HEALTH

Picture your body as a beautifully choreographed ballet, where hormones are the dancers gracefully moving in sync, maintaining the elegance of homeostasis. This balancing act is about achieving optimal hormone levels, that sweet spot where everything func-tions smoothly. Homeostasis, a fancy term for keeping the body's internal environment stable, is the ultimate goal. It's like the ther-mostat that keeps your home at a perfect temperature. When hormones are balanced, you have the energy to conquer the world, your mood is steady, and your sleep is as refreshing as a spa day.

However, just like in a ballet, many factors can disrupt this harmony. Age is a big one. As the years roll by, hormone production can change, sometimes leading to imbalances. Think of it as the body's way of saying, "Hey, I'm not as spry as I used to be!" Then there are the lifestyle choices. Diet, exercise, and sleep—or the lack thereof—play significant roles in how your hormones perform. Poor diet choices, sedentary habits, or sleep deprivation can throw the whole dance off balance. And let's not forget genetics. Some of us are simply predisposed to certain hormonal quirks, which can be as unpredictable as a toddler at a wedding.

Now, let's talk strategy. Maintaining hormonal balance is like keeping an engine in tune. First up, diet. Eating a balanced diet rich in whole foods can support hormonal harmony. Think colorful veggies, lean proteins, and healthy fats. Try to avoid processed foods and excessive sugars, as they can disrupt the balance. Stress management is another key player. Techniques such as meditation, deep breathing, or even walking in nature can keep stress hormones in check. Finally, regular physical activity is crucial. Exercise helps maintain a healthy weight and promotes the release of hormones like endorphins, which boost mood and energy levels.

But how do you know when your hormonal ballet is out of step? Pay attention to the signs. Fatigue and sleep disturbances are common indicators. If you find yourself hitting the snooze button one too many times, it might be a clue. Weight fluctuations without changes in diet or activity are another red flag. And let's not overlook mood instability. Feelings of irritability or anxiety that seem to come out of nowhere could be your hormones waving a little red flag.

Understanding and maintaining hormonal balance is like having a well-oiled machine. When everything works as it should, life feels a little more manageable, and you can focus on the things that matter most. So, next time you feel off-kilter, take a moment to consider your hormonal health. It might just be the key to getting back on track.

CHAPTER 2
SEX HORMONES UNSCRAMBLED

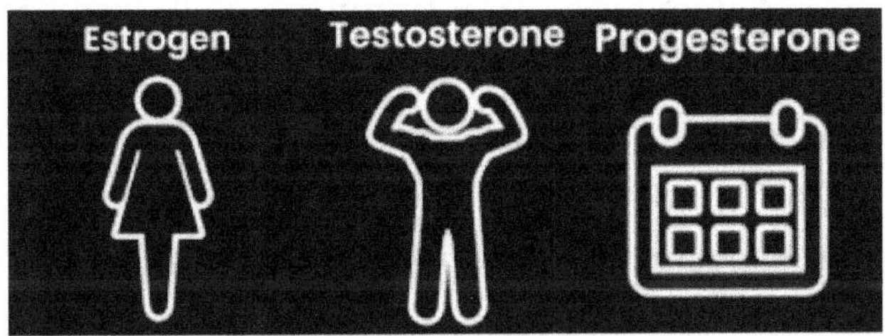

Imagine this: you're preparing for an exciting night out, looking fabulous in your favorite outfit. As you glance in the mirror for a final check, you notice a pesky pimple appearing out of nowhere. Or maybe you're just feeling unexplainably moody. More often than not, the culprit is estrogen, playing its part in the intricate drama of your bodily functions. Estrogen is usually considered the star player in women's health, but it doesn't just hang out in feminine circles. Men, it's in your corner, too, playing key roles you might not expect.

Estrogen is like the fairy godmother of the female reproductive system, waving its wand to make sure everything runs smoothly.

According to the Cleveland Clinic, it's responsible for regulating the menstrual cycle, ensuring that the monthly ritual is as drama-free as possible. This hormone helps the ovaries function properly and plays a huge role in fertility and conception. Without estrogen, the ovaries would be like a band with no lead singer, leading to all sorts of reproductive chaos. But estrogen's influence doesn't stop at reproduction. It also plays a crucial role in maintaining bone density. Consider it your body's secret weapon against osteoporosis, ensuring your bones remain as strong as your morning coffee.

Additionally, estrogen works in the background to offer cardiovascular protection, helping to keep those arteries clear and the heart beating like a well-tuned drum. Estrogen also plays a crucial role in brain development for cognitive functions like memory, learning, and problem-solving. Estrogen plays a vital role in maintaining collagen levels in the body, as it helps stimulate collagen production and supports skin elasticity. When estrogen levels decline, particularly perimenopause, the reduction in collagen can lead to signs of aging, such as wrinkles and sagging skin. This connection underscores the importance of estrogen not just for reproductive health but also for maintaining youthful, resilient skin.

Now, let's not forget about the fellas. While testosterone tends to hog the spotlight, estrogen is quietly doing its thing. In men, estrogen contributes to maintaining bone health and plays a part in libido and sexual function, according to the Cleveland Clinic. It's like the unsung hero working alongside testosterone to keep things balanced. Ensuring healthy levels of estrogen can even aid in reducing the risk of certain health issues, like heart disease.

So, how do you keep this mighty hormone in check? First, let's briefly talk about diet. Phytoestrogens, found in foods like soy and flaxseeds, can mimic estrogen in the body. These plant-based compounds can be a double-edged sword, acting as both a friend and foe, depending on your body's needs. Incorporating them gently into your diet can help maintain balance, but it's always wise to consult with a healthcare provider, especially if you're considering supplements. On the medical front, hormone replacement therapy (HRT) can be an option, particularly for those dealing with significant imbalances, but it's not without its considerations. Always weigh the benefits and risks with your doctor to ensure it's the right path for you.

Reflection Section: Discover Your Estrogen Allies

- Journaling Prompt: Spend a week noting your mood, energy levels, and any physical changes you observe. Do you notice any patterns or triggers that might relate to hormonal fluctuations?
- Food Checklist: Explore incorporating foods rich in phytoestrogens into your meals. Try recipes with tofu, flaxseeds, and chickpeas, and see how they impact your well-being.
- Consultation Reminder: Consider scheduling a check-up with your healthcare provider to discuss your hormonal health. Bring this book along and share what you've learned!

Estrogen is more than just a hormone; it's a vital component of your overall health, quietly orchestrating balance and well-being. Whether you're a woman navigating the complexities of your cycle or a man looking to maintain bone health, understanding estrogen's role can empower you to take charge of your hormonal health.

UNLEASHING THE BEAST: THE POWER OF TESTOSTERONE

Ah, testosterone—the hormone that often gets credited for transforming gangly teenagers into broad-shouldered adults, and for good reason. It's the key player in developing distinctly masculine features like increased muscle mass, deeper voices, and the ability to grow a beard that rivals a logger's. But it's not just about making you look like you could chop wood in a single swing. Testosterone significantly impacts muscle mass and strength, so gym-goers often talk about boosting their "T levels." It helps in muscle protein synthesis, meaning it aids your muscles in growing and getting stronger. And let's not forget about the voice deepening during adolescence. Testosterone causes the vocal cords to thicken, so that squeaky teen voice finally settles into something more baritone. Hair growth patterns? Yup, testosterone is behind that, too, influencing everything from the hair on your head to the fuzz on your face.

But, fellas, don't think this hormone is strictly your domain. Ladies have testosterone, too, and it plays a pivotal role in their health. For women, testosterone is crucial for maintaining energy levels and sexual health. It acts like a natural energy drink, helping you feel more vibrant and alive. Libido enhancement is one of its perks, keeping things interesting in the romance department. And yes, it also contributes to muscle tone and strength, so even women hit the weights to keep those muscles in top shape. So, while testosterone might be known as the "male hormone," it's also a vital part of female health.

Of course, like any good thing, balance is crucial. Testosterone imbalances can wreak havoc on both genders. Low testosterone levels in men might lead to symptoms like fatigue, decreased libido, and even mood swings that make you wonder if someone swapped your morning coffee for decaf. Ladies might experience similar symptoms, muscle weakness, and changes in menstrual cycles. On the flip side, high testosterone levels can lead to issues such as acne and increased body hair in women and even aggression and mood swings in men. Stress, poor nutrition, and lack of physical activity are common culprits behind these imbalances. So, how can you keep your testosterone levels in check?

Let's talk about natural ways to boost those testosterone levels. First up, resistance training. Lifting weights isn't just for bodybuilders; it can increase testosterone production. Think of it as giving your body a gentle nudge to produce more of the good stuff. Adequate sleep is another key player. During deep sleep, your body releases the most testosterone, so don't skimp on those Z's. Aim for 7-9 hours to keep your levels optimal. And let's not forget about nutrition. Foods rich in zinc and vitamin D, like eggs and fortified cereals, can help support testosterone production. These nutrients act like the building blocks for testosterone, so make sure your diet includes them.

THE CALMING QUEEN: ALL ABOUT PROGESTERONE

Progesterone is like the soothing balm of the hormonal world, quietly working behind the scenes to ensure everything runs smoothly. When it comes to reproduction, progesterone is the unsung hero. It plays a pivotal role during the luteal phase of the menstrual cycle, the time between ovulation and the start of your next period. It's the last phase of your 4 phase menstrual cycle. Let's hit the pause button for a second. Lets take a quick peek on these phases for those who aren't familiar with them or wouldn't mind a refresher.

- *Phase 1: Menstruation, the start of your period. Usually, three to seven days*
- *Phase 2: Follicular phase; this one also starts with day one of your menstrual cycle and ends at ovulation*
- *Phase 3: Ovulation-which is around day 13-15, is the release of an egg from your ovaries*
- *Phase 4: Lueal phase- which starts around day 19 and lasts until your cycle begins again.*

Now, back to progesterone.

Think of progesterone as the stage manager, ensuring the uterine lining is ready and welcoming for a potential pregnancy. If conception occurs, progesterone ensures the environment is just right for the embryo to implant and grow. It thickens the uterine lining, making it lush and nutrient-rich, like preparing a cozy nest for a new life. Without adequate levels of progesterone, this stage could be as chaotic as a last-minute wedding, with everything promising but nothing entirely prepared.

But beyond reproduction, progesterone wields its calming influence in ways that might surprise you. This hormone has neuroprotective effects, acting somewhat like a gentle therapist for your brain. It plays a crucial role in mood regulation and helps reduce anxiety, making it easier to face the day's challenges without feeling like you want to hide under a rock. Some studies suggest progesterone may help protect against neurological disorders, giving it an even more significant role in your overall mental health toolkit. The next time you feel inexplicably anxious or moody, consider that it might just be your progesterone levels acting up, like a smoke detector going off because of burnt toast.

Men might think they have no horse in the progesterone race, but that's not entirely true. Progesterone also plays a part in male health, although its role is less publicized. In men, progesterone acts as a precursor to testosterone, making it an essential part of the hormonal balance equation. Its anti-inflammatory properties also come in handy, helping to ward off various health issues that could arise from unchecked inflammation. So, men, next time you lift a weight or feel that post-workout glow, give a nod to progesterone—it's been quietly helping out.

Maintaining balanced progesterone levels is crucial for both genders; fortunately, there are natural ways to support this. Herbal supplements like chasteberry have long been used to promote hormonal balance, acting as nature's little helpers to boost progesterone levels. They're like the herbal equivalent of a warm cup of tea on a cold day, soothing and balancing. Managing stress is another effective way to keep progesterone in check. Chronic stress can lead to elevated cortisol levels, which in turn can suppress progesterone production. So, whether meditation, yoga, or simply taking a long walk, finding ways to decompress can help keep your hormonal balance in harmony.

As we wrap up our chat about progesterone, remember that this calming queen is more than just a player in the reproductive game —it's a vital part of your emotional and physical well-being. By understanding and supporting your progesterone levels, you're taking a significant step towards a balanced and healthy life. And with that, we move on to explore the dynamic world of metabolic hormones, where insulin, glucagon, and others take the stage to keep your energy levels in check.

CHAPTER 3
MASTERING METABOLIC HORMONES

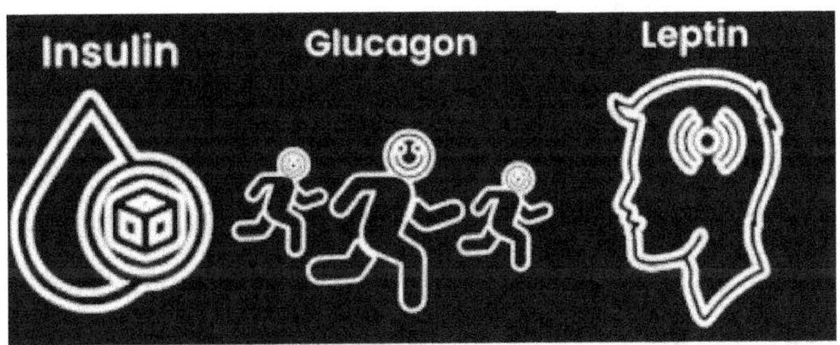

Imagine you're at a bustling airport. Planes are taking off, landing, and taxiing, and somehow, it all seems to work seamlessly. Now, picture insulin as the air traffic controller, coordinating the landing of glucose into your cells. Without insulin, glucose would be like a plane circling endlessly, unable to find a place to land. This hormone, secreted by the beta cells of the pancreas, plays a crucial role in managing the airport that is in your bloodstream by regulating blood glucose levels and ensuring your body stores energy efficiently. When you eat, insulin signals cells to open up and let glucose in, which is either used for energy or stored as glycogen in the liver and muscles for later use. It's like storing leftovers from a big dinner, ready to be reheated when needed.

However, when the system encounters a jam, the consequences can be severe. Insulin resistance, the unwelcome guest that overstays its welcome, leads to a buildup of glucose in the blood, akin to planes piling up on the runway. This resistance is a precursor to type 2 diabetes, a condition that affects millions globally. Obesity, particularly around the abdomen, is a frequent contributor to this issue. Chronic inflammation, often a silent partner in crime, worsens the situation by disrupting insulin's action. Think of inflammation as a disruptive passenger, causing delays and chaos.

You can make some lifestyle changes to get your insulin sensitivity back on track. First, consider the glycemic index of foods. Choosing low-glycemic options, like oatmeal or sweet potatoes, can help regulate blood sugar levels and prevent spikes. Regular physical activity is another powerful tool. Exercise increases insulin sensitivity, making your muscles more efficient at using glucose. It's like oiling the gears of a machine, ensuring everything runs smoothly. Don't underestimate the power of sleep and stress management, either. Adequate rest and relaxation reduce cortisol levels, which can improve insulin sensitivity. Imagine stress as turbulence; by calming it, you make the flight a lot smoother.

Innovations in insulin management are taking off, with new therapies and technologies on the horizon. Continuous glucose monitors (CGMs) provide real-time data, allowing for better control and management of blood sugar levels. These devices are like having a personal flight tracker, giving you the information needed to adjust your course.

Reflection Section: Check Your Insulin Sensitivity

- Journaling Prompt: Track your meals for a week, noting how you feel after eating different foods. Pay attention to energy levels and mood, looking for patterns related to blood sugar levels.
- Food Checklist: Experiment with low-glycemic foods. Swap white rice for quinoa or pasta for zucchini noodles, and observe any changes in how you feel throughout the day.
- Sleep and Stress Check: Reflect on your sleep quality and stress levels. Consider incorporating a relaxing bedtime routine or drinking a hot cup of chamomile tea before bed to help relax you.

Understanding insulin's role in your body is like learning to pilot your own plane. With the proper knowledge and tools, you can navigate your metabolic health with confidence and clarity. As technology and research continue to evolve, managing insulin levels becomes more accessible, empowering you to take control of your health in new and exciting ways. This understanding gives you the power to make informed decisions about your health, putting you in the driver's seat of your metabolic health journey.

SUGAR LIBERATION: GLUCAGON'S ROLE IN METABOLISM

Think of your body as a finely tuned car. While insulin is busy refueling the tank, glucagon is like the mechanic making sure you've got enough gas to keep going when you're on the road, far from a gas station. This hormone, produced by the alpha cells in your pancreas, plays a critical role in keeping your body's energy levels stable by releasing stored energy when you're not eating. When your blood sugar levels drop, glucagon kicks into action, promoting glycogenolysis. This is a process where glycogen, the stored form of glucose in your liver, is broken down to release glucose into the bloodstream. It's like finding a hidden stash of snacks when you're feeling a bit peckish. But glucagon doesn't stop there. It also triggers gluconeogenesis, a fancy term for creating new glucose from non-carbohydrate sources like amino acids. So, even when your pantry seems bare, glucagon ensures your cells aren't left starving.

The interplay between insulin and glucagon is a beautiful dance, ensuring that your body always has a steady supply of energy. When you eat a meal, insulin is released to help store the nutrients. But when you're fasting, glucagon steps in to maintain glucose levels, preventing you from feeling like a car stalled on the side of the highway. These two hormones work in a yin-yang fashion, balancing each other out through hormonal feedback mechanisms. When insulin levels rise after eating, glucagon is suppressed, and vice versa when you need to tap into those energy reserves. This balance is crucial, especially during different states like fasting and feeding. During fasting, glucagon ensures your body keeps running smoothly by maintaining glucose levels, preventing you from feeling like you're running on empty.

Glucagon, in addition to its other roles, is a key player in weight management, adding another tool to your metabolic toolkit. It promotes lipolysis, the breakdown of fats into energy, mobilizing those stubborn fat reserves that refuse to budge. Think of it as glucagon cracking open the vault where your body stashes fat, allowing you to use it as fuel. It also helps regulate appetite, signaling to your brain when you've had enough, which can be particularly helpful in maintaining a healthy weight. By influencing energy expenditure, glucagon can turn your metabolism into a more efficient engine, burning through calories and fat with greater ease.

Supporting healthy glucagon levels doesn't require a Ph.D. in nutrition. Simple lifestyle tweaks can go a long way. Intermittent fasting, for example, can naturally boost glucagon production. By creating longer periods between meals, your body learns to utilize stored energy efficiently, and glucagon becomes your best ally. High-protein diets also support glucagon function, as proteins help maintain glucose levels by providing a steady release of energy. So, think about adding more lean meats, beans, and nuts to your meals, turning your kitchen into a glucagon-friendly zone. These simple changes can make a significant difference in your metabolic health, and they're easy to incorporate into your daily routine.

THE SATIETY STAR: MEET LEPTIN

Picture leptin as the traffic cop in your brain, directing the flow of hunger and fullness signals with the precision of a maestro. This hormone, primarily produced by your body's fat cells, plays the leading role in regulating appetite and signaling satiety. When your fat stores are ample, leptin levels rise, sending a message to your hypothalamus—the brain's command center for hunger—that it's time to put down the fork and step away from the buffet. Essentially, leptin tells your brain, "We're good on reserves; no need for extra trips to the snack cupboard." It's the body's way of maintaining energy balance, ensuring you don't consume more fuel than you need. This feedback loop helps suppress hunger signals, making it easier to resist the siren call of that extra slice of cake or late-night snack.

However, the leptin system isn't foolproof. Enter leptin resistance, where the brain doesn't respond properly to leptin's signals, similar to ignoring a stop sign. This can lead to increased appetite and overeating despite having sufficient energy reserves. It's like constantly refilling a gas tank that's already full. High-fat diets, particularly those rich in saturated fats, have been shown to dampen leptin sensitivity. Over time, this blurs the communication between leptin and the brain, much like a bad phone connection that keeps cutting out. Genetic factors also play a role, with some individuals inheriting a predisposition to leptin resistance. This resistance is a significant player in the development of obesity and metabolic syndrome, creating a vicious cycle of weight gain and hormonal imbalance.

Fortunately, there are ways to enhance leptin sensitivity and support weight management. A balanced macronutrient intake is key. Aim for meals that include a healthy mix of carbohydrates, proteins, and fats, which can help regulate leptin levels effectively. Regular exercise is another powerful ally. Physical activity not only helps burn calories but also improves leptin sensitivity. It's like giving your leptin receptors a tune-up, ensuring they're in top working order. Engaging in both aerobic activities, like walking or cycling, and resistance training can have a synergistic effect, boosting your overall metabolic health.

On the research front, scientists are exploring exciting new avenues for leptin-related therapies. The development of leptin analogs—molecules that mimic leptin's action—offers potential for treating leptin resistance and associated conditions. These analogs could help bypass the resistance, allowing the body to respond to satiety signals more effectively. Leptin's role in inflammatory processes is also under investigation. Studies suggest that leptin may influence inflammation, which opens up possibilities for therapeutic interventions in inflammatory diseases. This research highlights leptin's multifaceted nature, going beyond appetite regulation to potentially impacting a range of health issues.

As we wrap up our exploration of metabolic hormones, it's clear that understanding these hormonal players can provide a wealth of insights into managing our health. From insulin and glucagon to leptin, each hormone contributes to the intricate dance of metabolism, influencing everything from energy levels to body weight. By paying attention to these signals and making informed lifestyle choices, you can work with your body rather than against it. With the basics of metabolic hormones under your belt, it's time to shift gears and explore how stress hormones play their part in the symphony of your body's functions.

CHAPTER 4
THE STRESS SQUAD: MEET ADRENALINE, CORTISOL, AND NOREPINEPHRINE

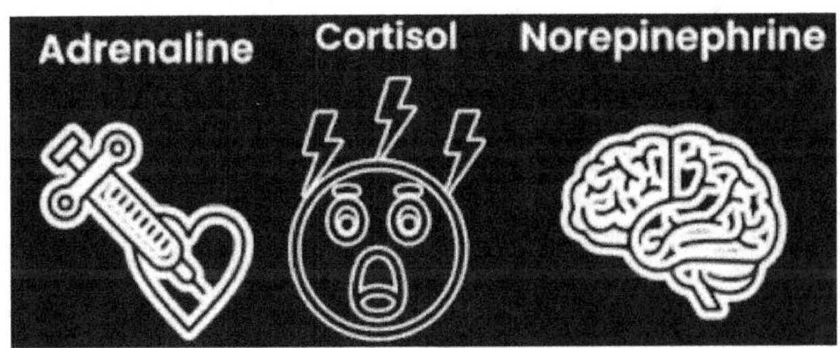

Picture this: it's Monday morning, your alarm didn't go off, and you're late for work. Your heart's racing, your palms are sweaty, and you're pretty sure you're about to meet your demise at the hands of your boss. Cue adrenaline, the unsung hero in your body's emergency response team.

Adrenaline, often referred to as epinephrine in the scientific world, is like your body's personal superhero, swooping in to save the day when things get scary. Released by the adrenal glands, adrenaline surges in response to stress, whether it's a saber-toothed tiger or just your mother-in-law coming over unannounced. Its primary role is activating the fight-or-flight response, that ancient survival mechanism that decides whether you should run like the wind or stand your ground. When adrenaline floods your system, your heart rate jumps, blood rushes to your muscles, and your pupils dilate to let in more light. It's like your body suddenly got a turbo boost, ready to tackle whatever challenge lies ahead.

The immediate effects of this hormone are pretty remarkable. By increasing heart rate and blood flow to muscles, adrenaline enhances alertness and focus, allowing you to think quickly and act decisively. It's the reason you might find yourself suddenly able to recall your third-grade teacher's name during a trivia game or sprint to catch a bus with the agility of an Olympic athlete. Adrenaline improves physical performance, making you feel like you could lift a car if needed (though maybe it's best to leave that to the professionals). In short bursts, adrenaline is your ally, sharpening your senses and preparing you for action.

However, what happens when this superpower is overused? Chronic exposure to adrenaline can turn from helpful to harmful, becoming more of a villain than a hero. Sustained high levels can lead to hypertension and cardiovascular strain, making your heart work overtime. According to the article "How adrenaline can be a heart breaker," prolonged adrenaline exposure can negatively impact heart health, causing issues like high blood pressure and increasing the risk of heart attacks. It can also manifest as anxiety and restlessness, leaving you feeling like a jittery squirrel who's had too much coffee. When your body is constantly on high alert, it eventually takes a toll, leading to a host of stress-related health problems.

Fortunately, you can manage adrenaline levels by incorporating simple techniques into your daily life. Breathing exercises and relaxation methods are effective at calming the adrenaline storm. Try taking slow, deep breaths in through your nose and out through your mouth, picturing yourself relaxing on a beach somewhere instead of stressing over Uncle Bob's latest conspiracy theory. Mindfulness practices, like meditation or yoga, can help you stay grounded and reduce stress, keeping adrenaline from running the show. These practices encourage you to focus on the present moment, helping to lower stress levels and reduce unnecessary adrenaline release.

Reflection Section: Take a Breather

- Breathing Exercise: To manage stress, try this simple exercise: Breathe in slowly through your nose for a count of four, hold for four, and exhale through your mouth for six. Repeat this for a few minutes whenever you feel stressed.
- Mindful Moment: Schedule a five-minute mindfulness break into your day. Find a quiet spot, close your eyes, and focus on your breath. Notice the rise and fall of your chest, and let go of any racing thoughts.

Understanding adrenaline's role in your body is like discovering the off switch on a particularly annoying alarm clock. By learning how to manage this powerful hormone, you can take control of your health, decrease stress, and maybe even enjoy your mother-in-law's visits just a little bit more. It's a feeling of empowerment, knowing that you have the tools to manage your body's response to stress.

SURVIVAL MODE: UNDERSTANDING CORTISOL'S ROLE

Imagine you're an actor in a never-ending thriller movie, where the plot twist is always lurking around the corner. That's the role cortisol plays in your life—your body's own suspense director, constantly preparing you for action. Cortisol, often dubbed the "stress hormone," is produced by the adrenal glands and has a starring role in managing how your body handles stress. But don't let its reputation fool you; cortisol is also crucial for regulating blood sugar levels. It ensures you have enough energy to tackle the day by balancing the glucose in your bloodstream. When stress hits, cortisol is released, prompting the liver to produce more glucose. This extra sugar acts like a quick energy snack, helping you respond efficiently to stressful situations. However, cortisol suppresses the immune system during prolonged stress, leaving you more vulnerable to colds and other illnesses. It's as if cortisol tells your immune system to take a coffee break just when you might need it most.

While cortisol can be a lifesaver in small, manageable doses, chronic stress can lead to cortisol overload. This is when the trouble starts. Prolonged high cortisol levels can lead to a host of health issues that you definitely don't want on your resume. One significant consequence is weight gain, particularly around the abdominal area. It's like cortisol draws a bullseye on your midsection, inviting fat cells to settle there. This isn't just about aesthetics—excess belly fat is linked to higher risks of metabolic disorders and heart disease.

Moreover, cortisol can impair cognitive functions and memory, leaving you feeling like you're trying to think through a thick fog. Have you ever walked into a room and forgotten why you were there? Chronic cortisol exposure can amplify those moments, making you wonder if you've misplaced your memory along with your keys.

Cortisol follows a daily rhythm, dancing in tune with your body's internal clock. Typically, cortisol levels surge in the morning, giving you that "rise and shine" energy boost as you greet the day. It's like having a natural shot of espresso to get you going. As the day progresses, cortisol levels gradually decline, hitting their lowest point in the evening, setting the stage for a restful night's sleep. Maintaining this natural rhythm is vital for overall health and wellness. Disruptions to this cycle, such as staying up late or constant stress, can throw your cortisol levels off balance, making you feel perpetually tired yet wired. Sleep disturbances, weight gain, and mood swings become all too familiar when your cortisol rhythm is out of sync.

Thankfully, you can take action to keep your cortisol levels in check. Regular physical activity is a fantastic way to modulate cortisol. Exercise acts like a reset button, helping to regulate cortisol levels and reduce stress. Aim for a mix of aerobic activities and strength training to get the most benefits. A balanced diet rich in adequate protein and healthy fats can also support healthy cortisol levels. Foods like avocados, nuts, and oily fish provide essential nutrients that help your body manage stress more effectively.

Additionally, establishing good sleep hygiene practices is crucial. Create a relaxing bedtime routine, limit screen time before bed, and ensure your sleep environment is conducive to rest. These practices help maintain your natural cortisol rhythm, allowing for a more restful sleep and a better start to your day.

THE CALM AND ALERT HORMONE: BALANCING WITH NOREPINEPHRINE

Norepinephrine, often overshadowed by its more famous cousins like adrenaline, plays a crucial role in both stress response and attention. Imagine it as the conductor of an orchestra, ensuring that all parts of your brain and body are in sync. When you're faced with stress, norepinephrine steps up to enhance your vigilance, making sure you're keenly aware of your surroundings. It kicks your senses into high gear, like a camera suddenly shifting into focus, allowing you to process information quickly and accurately. This heightened state of alertness is what enables you to react swiftly in stressful situations, ensuring you're ready to tackle whatever life throws your way. However, norepinephrine doesn't just shine during stress; it also plays a pivotal role in maintaining attention and focus during everyday tasks. Whether you're deciphering a complex spreadsheet at work or trying to follow a recipe without burning dinner, norepinephrine is there, helping you stay on task and keeping distractions at bay.

But norepinephrine's influence extends beyond just keeping you alert and focused; it also plays a significant role in your emotional health. This hormone is intimately linked to mood regulation and emotional responses. High levels of norepinephrine are associated with feelings of anxiety and stress, almost as if your body is constantly on edge, waiting for the next shoe to drop. On the flip side, low levels of this hormone can contribute to depression, leaving you feeling as though you're trudging through life with a perpetual rain cloud overhead. It's a balancing act, and when norepinephrine levels are just right, you find yourself in a sweet spot where emotions are stable and mood swings are minimal.

This balance is crucial for overall mental health, ensuring that you can navigate life's ups and downs with a steady hand and a clear mind.

So, how can you achieve this balance and keep norepinephrine levels in check? Cognitive-behavioral techniques are a great place to start. These strategies help rewire negative thought patterns and reduce stress, which in turn can help regulate norepinephrine levels. Think of it as a mental tune-up, ensuring that your engine runs smoothly and efficiently. The diet also plays a role, particularly in foods rich in tyrosine, a precursor to norepinephrine. Incorporating foods like turkey, cheese, and nuts into your meals can support the production of this hormone, providing your brain with the raw materials it needs to stay alert and balanced.

Innovations in norepinephrine management are also making strides in the scientific community. Recent research is exploring pharmacological interventions that target norepinephrine pathways, offering potential treatments for anxiety and depression. These therapies aim to fine-tune norepinephrine levels, providing relief for those struggling with mood disorders. Neurofeedback and biofeedback techniques are also gaining traction as effective methods for managing stress and emotional responses. By monitoring physiological signals like heart rate and brain waves, these techniques help individuals achieve better control over their body's stress response, promoting a sense of calm and well-being.

As we wrap up our exploration of stress and adrenal hormones, it's clear that understanding these hormonal players is critical to managing stress and maintaining mental health. From adrenaline's quick burst of energy to cortisol's daily rhythm and norepinephrine's dual role in focus and emotion, each hormone plays a unique part in the complex dance of your body's stress response. By learning to balance these hormones, you can take control of your health, improve your well-being, and face life's challenges confidently. Now, let's turn the page and dive into the fascinating world of appetite and digestive hormones, where your body's hunger and fullness signals take center stage.

CHAPTER 5
APPETITE AND DIGESTIVE HORMONES

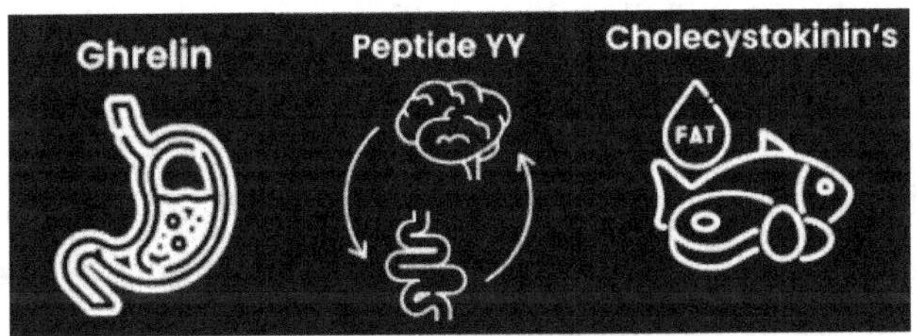

Picture this: you're sitting at your desk, working diligently, when suddenly, your stomach growls with the ferocity of a lion. You glance at the clock, and it's only been an hour since breakfast. What gives? Meet ghrelin, the "hunger hormone," playing its part in this all-too-familiar scenario. Ghrelin is like a mischievous little gremlin that lives in your stomach, whispering to your brain when it's time to eat. It's produced primarily in the stomach and sends signals to the brain's hypothalamus, the command center for hunger. When your stomach is empty, ghrelin levels rise, and your brain gets the memo to start thinking about your next meal. It's why you might find yourself daydreaming about pizza during a boring meeting.

But ghrelin isn't just a one-trick pony. Its influence extends to how you eat and how your body manages energy. When ghrelin levels are elevated, your appetite increases, prompting you to start seeking out food like a heat-seeking missile. It stimulates appetite and encourages food-seeking behavior, often making you reach for snacks even when you're not truly hungry. Ever find yourself opening the fridge just to see what's there? That's ghrelin nudging you along. It also plays a role in meal initiation, signaling to your body that it's time to chow down. This hormone essentially tells you it's okay to have that second breakfast or to indulge in a late-night snack, making meal timing a bit of a free-for-all.

Ghrelin doesn't just make you hungry; it also affects energy balance and body weight regulation. It influences energy intake and expenditure, not just the quantity of food you eat but also how your body burns those calories. Ghrelin levels can impact your body mass index (BMI), playing a part in the complex dance of weight management. Higher ghrelin levels are often found in people trying to lose weight, making it challenging to keep those pounds off. It's like trying to win a tug-of-war with your own body, where ghrelin is cheering on the other side.

So, how can you manage this hunger hormone? It turns out lifestyle and dietary changes can help keep ghrelin in check. High-protein meals are particularly effective at suppressing ghrelin, so consider adding more protein-rich foods like chicken, beans, or Greek yogurt to your diet. Protein creates a longer-lasting feeling of fullness, helping to keep those hunger pangs at bay. But that's not all. Sleep also plays a crucial role in ghrelin regulation. Lack of sleep can lead to increased ghrelin levels, making you hungrier and more prone to overeating. By aiming for 7-9 hours of sleep per night, you can keep ghrelin levels balanced and avoid that midnight snack attack, staying informed and in control of your hunger.

Reflection Section: Hunger Games

Mindful Eating Exercise: Next time you feel the urge to snack, pause and ask yourself if you're truly hungry or if ghrelin is just having a little fun. This simple exercise empowers you to rate your hunger on a scale from 1 to 10, and consider if a glass of water or a quick walk might satisfy the urge instead. By practicing mindful eating, you can take back control from ghrelin and make more conscious food choices.Understanding ghrelin and its influence on hunger and energy balance can help you take control of your eating habits. By making mindful choices and incorporating dietary changes, you can keep this hunger hormone in check, helping you achieve your health and wellness goals.

GUT INSTINCTS: UNDERSTANDING PEPTIDE YY

Imagine sitting down after a delightful meal, feeling comfortably full and satisfied. That sensation isn't just the product of good conversation and tasty food; it's partly due to peptide YY, or PYY, doing its thing behind the scenes. This nifty hormone is released by cells in the ileum and colon right after you've polished off your plate. Once released, peptide YY heads straight to the brain, acting like a traffic cop directing the flow of your appetite. It sends signals to the brain's hunger center, effectively telling it, "We're full, no more food needed right now!" This interaction helps reduce your appetite, making you feel less inclined to reach for that extra slice of cake.

Now, let's pause for a moment to explore the two hormones that send the message to your brain that you've had enough to eat and can stop. I'm sure you are thinking what I was thinking when I learned about this hormone. If peptide YY tells your brain that you're full and don't need to eat more, and then leptin also sends the message that you've had enough to eat, why are there two hormones that do the same job?

The answer is this: Leptin's main role is in managing long-term energy balance by signaling feelings of fullness based on the body's overall fat stores. Peptide YY works more immediately to curb appetite right after a meal, released mainly from the gut in response to food consumption. So, even though they both essentially perform the same role, there is a difference. I hope that helps clarify things—now, let's get back to Peptide YY.

Peptide YY doesn't just signal your brain to stop eating; it also plays a significant role in how your body digests and absorbs nutrients. One of its key functions is to slow down gastric emptying, ensuring the food you eat doesn't rush through your digestive system too quickly. This allows your body more time to absorb all those essential nutrients. It's like giving your stomach a chance to savor the meal, ensuring nothing goes to waste. This process also helps stabilize your blood sugar levels, preventing peaks and crashes that can turn you into a hangry monster.

Now, let's talk about peptide YY's potential role in weight management. With obesity being a growing concern worldwide, researchers are looking at peptide YY as a possible target for treatments. The idea is that by boosting peptide YY levels, we might be able to suppress appetite more effectively and assist with weight loss. Some clinical trials have explored using peptide YY analogs —synthetic versions of the hormone—to curb hunger. While the research is still ongoing, early findings suggest that increasing peptide YY might be a promising strategy for managing obesity. This potential breakthrough offers hope for a future where a simple hormone tweak could help keep those extra pounds at bay.

So, how can you naturally enhance your peptide YY levels? The good news is that certain dietary choices can help. High-fiber foods, like fruits, vegetables, and whole grains, are known to boost peptide YY secretion. These foods take longer to digest, keeping you fuller for longer and encouraging your body to produce more peptide YY . It's like giving your digestive system a gentle nudge to keep things balanced. Regular exercise is also a great way to increase peptide YY levels. Physical activity has been shown to stimulate the release of this satiety hormone, adding another reason to lace up those sneakers and get moving. Whether it's a brisk walk, a yoga session, or lifting weights, exercise can be a fantastic ally in managing hunger and supporting weight management.

Understanding how peptide YY works and its impact on your body can open up a world of possibilities for maintaining a healthy weight and enjoying a balanced diet. By making mindful food choices and incorporating regular exercise, you can positively influence peptide YY levels and take control of your appetite. Remember, it's not just about what you eat but how your body processes it.

DIGESTIVE DYNAMICS: CHOLECYSTOKININ'S (KOW·LUH·SI·STUH·KAI·NUHN) ROLE

Imagine you're at a gourmet restaurant, savoring a meal that's a symphony of flavors. Your digestive system is hard at work, and one of the key players in this culinary orchestra is cholecystokinin, or as we will refer to it as, CCK. Produced in the duodenum(doo·ow·dee·nuhm), the first section of the small intestine, CCK is like the maestro directing the symphony of digestion. Its primary role is to stimulate the release of digestive enzymes and bile, both crucial for breaking down the food you've just enjoyed. When food enters the small intestine, CCK is released, prompting the pancreas to secrete enzymes that disassemble proteins, carbohydrates, and fats into smaller, absorbable molecules. It's akin to a sous-chef prepping ingredients for the chef to create a masterpiece. Without CCK's signal, your body would struggle to extract the nutrients it needs from food.

Beyond its digestive duties, CCK plays a significant role in managing your appetite and satiety. After a meal, as CCK levels rise, it communicates with your brain to let it know that it's time to slow down on the eating. It's like an internal text message saying, "Hey, we're full down here!" This hormone helps regulate meal size by suppressing short-term appetite, ensuring you don't overeat. CCK also interacts with other satiety hormones, like leptin and peptide YY, forming a tag team that keeps your appetite in check. Together, they create a feedback loop that helps your body decide when enough is enough, curbing the temptation to have dessert right after dinner.

CCK has a special relationship with dietary fats, playing a crucial role in their digestion and absorption. When you eat fats, CCK signals the gallbladder to contract, releasing bile into the small intestine. Bile acts like a detergent, emulsifying fats and breaking them down into smaller droplets, which makes them easier to digest and absorb. This process is vital because fats are a dense source of energy and essential fatty acids, which your body needs for various functions, including hormone production. Without

CCK's intervention, fat digestion would be slow and inefficient, much like trying to dissolve oil in water without soap.

Supporting healthy CCK levels is all about balance and mindful eating. Including healthy fats in your diet, such as avocados, nuts, and olive oil, can promote CCK production and improve digestion. These fats not only taste great but also help you feel fuller for longer, reducing the urge to snack between meals. On the flip side, practicing mindful eating can enhance CCK's effectiveness. By taking the time to savor each bite, you allow your body to register fullness cues, preventing overeating properly. Slow down, enjoy your meals, and listen to your body's signals. This practice supports digestion and elevates your dining experience to a whole new level.

As we wrap up our exploration of appetite and digestive hormones, it's clear that understanding these hormonal players can transform your relationship with food. From ghrelin's hunger cues to peptide YY's satiety signals and CCK's digestive orchestration, each hormone plays a unique role in maintaining balance. By tuning into these signals and making mindful choices, you can support your digestive health and overall well-being. Next, we'll dig into the fascinating world of thyroid and growth hormones, exploring how they influence energy, metabolism, and development.

CHAPTER 6
THYROID AND GROWTH HORMONES

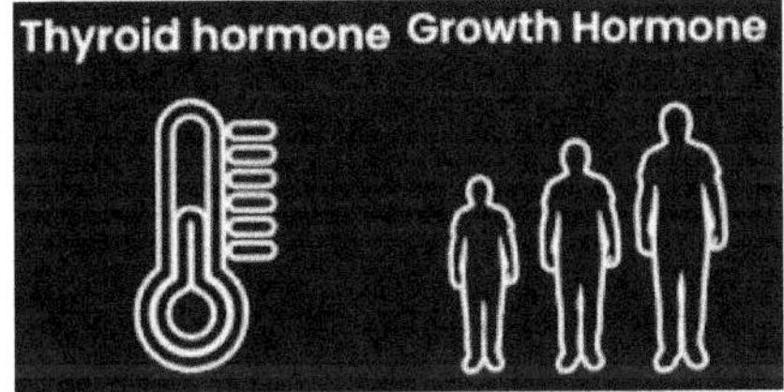

Picture this: you're powering through your day, fueled by nothing but pure determination and caffeine. Suddenly, you hit a wall. Not a literal one—let's hope your coordination is better than that—but an energy wall. You find yourself dragging, like a phone on its last 2% battery. What gives? Well, say hello to your thyroid gland, the tiny yet mighty butterfly-shaped powerhouse nestled in your neck. It's the unsung hero of energy regulation, making sure you're not just a couch potato or a jittery squirrel. The thyroid keeps things running smoothly thanks to its production of thyroid hormones, which include thyroxine (T4) and triiodothyronine (T3). These hormones are the ultimate multitaskers, regulating metabolism and ensuring you have enough energy to tackle even the most challenging days.

The process begins with the thyroid-stimulating hormone (TSH), the overzealous manager of this whole operation. Released by the pituitary gland, TSH tells the thyroid when to get busy making T3 and T4. Once released into the bloodstream, these hormones act like tiny messengers, zipping through your body to every cell, giving them the pep talk they need to convert food into energy. They ensure that your metabolism hums along like a well-oiled machine, ensuring you're not burning through calories too quickly or holding onto them like a squirrel hoarding nuts for winter. But that's not all—T3 and T4 also affect heart rate regulation, body temperature, and even cholesterol levels. It's like having a personal trainer, thermostat, and dietitian all rolled into one.

However, like any great system, things can go awry. Enter hypothyroidism and hyperthyroidism, the dramatic duo of thyroid imbalances. Hypothyroidism, or an underactive thyroid, slows everything down. Imagine trying to run a marathon through molasses. Symptoms like fatigue, weight gain, and sensitivity to cold make you feel like you're perpetually under a gray cloud. On the flip side, hyperthyroidism, where the thyroid goes into overdrive, can leave you feeling like a hummingbird on a sugar rush. Symptoms include rapid heart rate, weight loss, and a sensitivity to heat. It's like your internal thermostat is stuck on high, making you feel like you're living in a perpetual sauna. Both conditions can significantly impact your heart health and cholesterol levels, so it's crucial to keep an eye on these pesky imbalances.

So, how can you keep your thyroid in top shape? Let's talk nutrition. The thyroid loves iodine, and it's essential for hormone production. Foods like seaweed, fish, and dairy are great sources of iodine. But like everything, moderation is key—too much iodine can be as problematic as too little. Selenium is another crucial player that helps convert T4 into the more active T3. Brazil nuts and sunflower seeds are excellent sources, so maybe keep a stash handy for a healthy snack. But beware of goitrogens, substances found in certain raw vegetables like broccoli and kale, which can interfere with thyroid function. Goitrogens are compounds that can disrupt the production of thyroid hormones by interfering with iodine uptake in the thyroid gland. Cooking these veggies can help reduce their goitrogenic properties, so don't worry; you can still enjoy your green smoothies.

Keeping an eye on your thyroid health is essential, and regular monitoring can help catch any issues early. Blood tests measuring TSH, T3, and T4 levels are the gold standard for assessing thyroid function. Think of it as a routine tune-up for your body, ensuring everything runs smoothly. In some cases, a thyroid ultrasound might be needed to check for nodules or structural issues. It's a non-invasive way to get a closer look at what's happening in your neck. Regular check-ups with your healthcare provider can help ensure your thyroid remains in tip-top shape so you can keep living life at full throttle.

Understanding your thyroid's role in energy regulation and metabolism is like having a backstage pass to your body's inner workings. By supporting your thyroid through mindful dietary choices and regular health check-ups, you can keep this gland humming along, ensuring you're ready to tackle whatever life throws your way.

If you're interested in learning more about the thyroid, I have a whole book dedicated to it called The Small but Mighty Thyroid: Meet Your Tiny Queen of Health and Energy.

FUEL FOR GROWTH: THE BENEFITS OF GROWTH HORMONE

Growth hormone (GH) is like the body's secret sauce for growth and repair—think of it as the fairy dust that helps you grow taller and stronger. Produced by the pituitary gland, a small but powerful gland located at the base of the brain, this hormone promotes bone and muscle growth, making it crucial for our development from tiny tots to full-grown adults. The pituitary gland, often referred to as the 'master gland' because it controls the functions of other endocrine glands, releases GH in response to various signals from the body. Growth hormone is the reason kids sprout up seemingly overnight and why your muscles can recover after a grueling workout. It doesn't stop at growth, though. GH plays a pivotal role in regulating body composition, ensuring you maintain a healthy muscle and fat ratio. It does this by promoting protein synthesis, which helps build and repair muscles, and by influencing the metabolism of glucose and lipids. Essentially, GH helps your body use fats for fuel, preserving precious muscle tissue and ensuring you're as fit as a fiddle.

However, like any good thing, balance is key. Growth hormone deficiency can lead to some pretty noticeable issues, especially in children. Without enough GH, children may experience short stature and delayed growth, like a plant struggling to reach the sunlight. In adults, GH deficiency can result in muscle weakness and increased fat, making you feel like you're stuck in a sluggish rut. It's not just about aesthetics—these issues can affect your overall health and quality of life. On the flip side, too much GH can lead to conditions like acromegaly and gigantism, where the body grows excessively, leading to enlarged hands and feet and other health complications. Imagine feeling like you're outgrowing your own body; it can be both physically and emotionally challenging. Symptoms of acromegaly include enlarged hands and feet, facial changes such as a protruding jaw and enlarged nose, joint pain, and increased sweating. Gigantism, a condition that occurs when excess GH is produced during childhood, can lead to excessive growth and height. Recognizing these symptoms early can help in the timely management of these conditions.

If you're looking to boost your GH levels naturally, there are some lifestyle choices that can help. High-intensity interval training (HIIT) is a fantastic way to stimulate growth hormone release. These short bursts of intense exercise get your heart pumping and your GH flowing, helping you build muscle and burn fat more efficiently. Sleep is another critical factor. During the deep stages of sleep, your body releases the most GH, so don't skimp on those precious hours of rest. Aim for a solid seven to nine hours a night to optimize your GH levels. Intermittent fasting is another strategy that can enhance GH secretion. By creating more extended periods between meals, your body learns to use growth hormone more effectively, promoting fat loss and muscle gain.

Therapeutically, growth hormone has some fascinating uses, especially for those with a deficiency. In children with GH deficiency, GH therapy can help them reach their full growth potential, allowing them to grow at a more typical rate. It's like giving them a helping hand to reach the top shelf. For adults, GH therapy can be beneficial in treating muscle-wasting diseases, helping to preserve muscle mass and improve quality of life. However, the use of GH in anti-aging treatments remains a topic of controversy. While some believe it can help maintain a youthful appearance and vitality, others caution against its use due to potential side effects and ethical concerns. It's a debate that continues in the medical community, with research ongoing to determine the safest and most effective applications of GH therapy.

In the grand scheme of things, growth hormone is a crucial player in your body's health and well-being. Whether you're focused on building muscle, losing fat, or simply maintaining a healthy balance, GH plays a role. By understanding how this hormone works and how you can support it through lifestyle choices and, if necessary, medical intervention, you can take charge of your health and fitness. As we wrap up our chapter on growth and thyroid hormones, it's clear that these powerful hormones are central to our vitality and energy. Next, we'll explore the fascinating world of sleep and circadian rhythm hormones, where your body's internal clock keeps everything ticking smoothly.

CHAPTER 7
SLEEP AND CIRCADIAN RHYTHM HORMONES

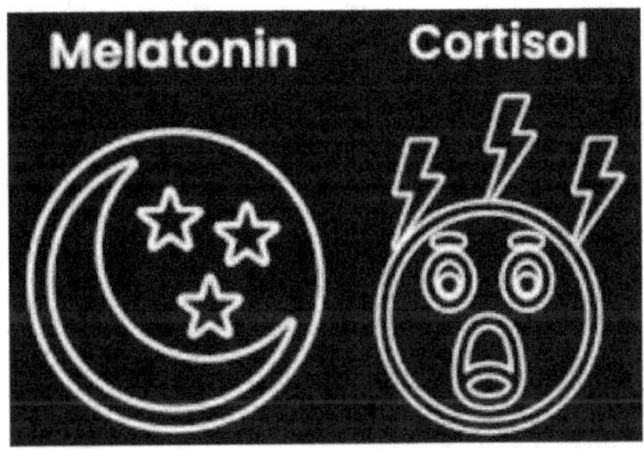

It's 3 a.m., and once again, you find yourself wide awake, scrolling through social media memes, contemplating life's mysteries. Meanwhile, your pillow gives you the silent treatment because you promised you'd be asleep by now. Sound familiar? You might be able to blame your friend melatonin—or rather, the lack thereof. Melatonin is the hormone that whispers sweet nothings to your brain, coaxing it into a peaceful slumber. Imagine it as your internal dimmer switch, gradually lowering the lights as night falls, preparing you for a restful sleep. But when this dimmer switch is jammed, you're left tossing, turning, and wondering why sheep-counting isn't working its magic.

Melatonin is produced by the pineal gland, a tiny pea-sized structure in your brain that has a big job. This hormone's production kicks into high gear in response to darkness, and that's where the magic begins. When night falls, your eyes detect this change in light, sending a message to the brain, specifically to the suprachiasmatic nucleus (SCN), the master clock of your circadian rhythm. The SCN, perched like a conductor in the orchestra of sleep, signals the pineal gland to start the melatonin production line. As melatonin levels rise, they send signals to the body that it's time to hit the hay, easing you into a state of relaxation and facilitating sleep onset. Light exposure, however, can throw a wrench in this process, as it suppresses melatonin production and can delay sleep, making those late-night Netflix binges a risky game.

The role of melatonin in regulating your sleep-wake cycle is akin to that of a seasoned air traffic controller, ensuring a smooth transition between sleep and wakefulness. It's a crucial player in adjusting your circadian rhythms, which follow a roughly 24-hour cycle and help synchronize your internal clock with the external environment. When melatonin levels peak during the night, they signal the body to wind down, promoting restful sleep. As morning approaches and light creeps in, melatonin levels naturally dip, giving way to wakefulness. This cycle keeps you in sync with the world, balancing your sleep and waking hours like a well-tuned grandfather clock. However, disruptions to this rhythm, such as shift work or jet lag, can leave you feeling like you've lost the beat, struggling with sleep disorders and fatigue.

As we age, melatonin doesn't quite keep up its youthful enthusiasm. By the time you're over 40, melatonin production often declines, leading to changes in sleep quality. It's as though your body's sleep orchestra is missing a few key players, resulting in a less harmonious performance. This decrease in melatonin can contribute to sleep disorders such as insomnia, leaving you counting sheep and pondering existential questions at 2 a.m. Older adults may find themselves waking up earlier than desired or experiencing fragmented sleep, contributing to daytime sleepiness and a host of other health issues. The decline in melatonin with age highlights the importance of understanding and supporting this hormone to maintain a good night's sleep.

Consider making a few lifestyle and environmental tweaks to optimize melatonin levels naturally. These changes have the potential to significantly improve your sleep quality. First, embrace the daylight. Exposure to natural light during the day can help regulate your circadian rhythm, promoting melatonin production when night falls. Think of it as giving your internal clock a nudge, reminding it to stay on schedule. As the sun sets, create a dark, cool sleeping environment to encourage melatonin release. Blackout curtains, a fan, and a cozy blanket can transform your bedroom into a sleep haven, signaling your body that it's time to wind down.

Avoiding blue light from screens before bedtime is also crucial. The light emitted by phones, tablets, and computers can wreak havoc on melatonin production, tricking your brain into thinking it's still daytime. Consider setting a digital curfew and giving your eyes a break at least an hour before sleep. If you find that natural methods aren't cutting it, melatonin supplements might be an option worth exploring. These supplements can help with specific sleep disorders, like jet lag or shift work-related sleep disruption. Still, it's wise to consult a healthcare provider before diving in, especially since these aren't FDA-approved.

Reflection Section: Melatonin Mastery

Sleep Environment Checklist: Transform your bedroom into a melatonin-friendly zone. Check for blackout curtains, a comfortable mattress, and the optimal room temperature. Evaluate your pre-sleep routine: are you limiting screen time, and do you have a relaxing bedtime ritual? Reflect on how these changes impact your sleep quality over the next week.

Understanding melatonin's role in your sleep cycle is not just informative, it's empowering. It equips you with the knowledge to make informed decisions about your sleep environment and habits, ultimately leading to better rest and improved well-being. With the right adjustments, you can harness the power of this vital hormone and enjoy the rejuvenating sleep you deserve.

RISE AND SHINE: THE ROLE OF CORTISOL IN WAKING UP

Picture this: You're nestled comfortably in your bed, dreaming of winning the lottery or eating your weight in chocolate. Suddenly, you're awake, and your to-do list is already in your face, waving frantically. Who's the culprit behind this rude awakening? Cortisol is your body's natural alarm clock. Remember back in chapter four, we learned about the stress hormones adrenaline, cortisol, and norepinephrine? And remember how I mentioned how cortisol levels surge in the morning, giving you that "rise and shine" energy boost as you greet the day. That's right; cortisol plays a role in the fight-or-flight hormone group and the sleep and circadian rhythm group.

Unlike that blaring clock on your nightstand, cortisol wakes you gently, preparing your body to greet the day with gusto. Cortisol has a reputation for being the bearer of bad news. But it's not all doom and gloom. In the morning, cortisol levels rise, giving you the energy boost you need to roll out of bed and face the world. The cortisol awakening response (CAR) process is like your body's version of a morning espresso shot, minus the caffeine jitters.

Cortisol follows a diurnal rhythm, meaning it has a predictable daily pattern. Levels peak in the morning, usually within 30 minutes of waking, giving you that "let's conquer the day" feeling. This peak is crucial for activating metabolism, ensuring your body has enough energy to start functioning after a night of fasting. Think of it as your body flipping the switch from "rest and digest" to "wake and energize." CAR doesn't just wake you up; it also enhances cognitive function and focus, making sure you remember where you left your keys and how to make a decent cup of coffee. It's like having a personal assistant whispering reminders and important facts into your ear as you go about your morning routine.

However, maintaining this natural cortisol rhythm is easier said than done. Modern life, with its chronic stressors, can throw cortisol levels out of whack, leading to a cascade of issues. Chronic stress keeps cortisol levels elevated, like a fire alarm that just won't quit. This can lead to sleep disturbances and fatigue, making you feel like a zombie in desperate need of a nap. Then there's shift work and irregular sleep schedules, which can further disrupt cortisol patterns, leaving you perpetually jet-lagged even if you haven't left your time zone. Imagine trying to keep time with a drummer who's playing a completely different song. It's no wonder you feel out of sync.

So, how can you restore balance to your cortisol levels and improve sleep quality and daytime performance? Start by establishing consistent sleep and wake times, even on weekends, when possible. This helps regulate your body's internal clock, keeping cortisol levels in check. Regularity is your friend here, so resist the temptation to snooze until noon on Saturdays. Stress management techniques like yoga and meditation can also work wonders for cortisol balance. By calming the mind and reducing stress, these practices help lower cortisol levels, making it easier to drift off at night and wake up refreshed in the morning. They're like a soothing lullaby for your hormones.

Morning exposure to natural light is another simple yet effective strategy. Sunlight helps reset your internal clock, signaling to your body that it's time to wake up and shine. It's like nature's very own wake-up call, and it's completely free. Try stepping outside for a morning walk or enjoying your breakfast by a sunny window. Limiting caffeine and sugar intake late in the day can also keep cortisol levels stable. While that afternoon coffee might seem like a good idea, it can interfere with your sleep cycle, making it harder to fall asleep at night. Opt for a decaf or herbal tea instead, and consider swapping sugary snacks for healthier alternatives. Your body—and your cortisol—will thank you for it.

Restoring cortisol balance is key to unlocking a more energized and focused day. With some simple lifestyle adjustments, you can keep this powerful hormone working in your favor rather than against you. As we wrap up our exploration of cortisol and its role in your wake-up routine, remember that understanding these natural rhythms can help you live a more balanced and fulfilling life. Next up, we'll dive into the world of emotional well-being, exploring how other key hormones influence your mood and mental health.

CHAPTER 8
HORMONES AND EMOTIONAL WELL-BEING

You know that feeling when you finally find your keys after searching for hours, and you experience that wave of relief and joy? You can thank dopamine for that little rush. It's like your brain's internal high-five, rewarding you for a job well done. Dopamine is the star player in our brain's reward system, acting as both the cheerleader and the coach, driving motivation and pleasure. When you accomplish something—be it finding those elusive keys or tasting that first sip of morning coffee—dopamine is there to say, "Well done, you!" It's a key neurotransmitter, a chemical messenger that zips around your brain, influencing your feelings and behavior.

Dopamine operates through intricate pathways in your brain, mainly the dopaminergic (dow-puh-muh-nur-juhk) pathways. Imagine these pathways as a network of roads, with dopamine being the eager traveler exploring every corner. It's most famously associated with the mesolimbic (meh-suh-lim-buhk) pathway. This circuit runs from the ventral tegmental area (VTA) to the nucleus accumbens and is central to the concept of reward prediction and reinforcement. Let's briefly break down the VTA before moving on for better understanding.

The ventral tegmental area (VTA) is a midbrain structure involved in multiple behaviors and mental states, including:

- **Reward and Motivation:** The VTA houses dopamine neurons essential for reward processing, reinforcement, and emotional arousal.
- **Addiction and Depression:** Serving as a central hub, the VTA plays a significant role in addiction and depressive disorders.
- **Schizophrenia:** The VTA is associated with schizophrenia and other neuropsychiatric conditions.
- **Executive Function:** It also contributes to executive functions, such as decision-making and self-regulation.

Now, let's get back to the reward hormone, dopamine.

Think of dopamine as your brain's personal crystal ball, always anticipating which activities will bring pleasure or satisfaction and encouraging you to repeat them. Whether it's the satisfaction of a successful project at work or the delight of a good meal, dopamine reinforces these behaviors by rewarding you with a feel-good buzz.

The influence of dopamine extends far beyond just making you feel good. It plays a crucial role in mood regulation and decision-making. Have you ever found yourself reaching for that second slice of cake or buying a pair of shoes you don't really need? That's dopamine whispering in your ear, urging you toward pleasure-seeking activities. Unfortunately, this can sometimes lead to risky behavior, as dopamine loves a thrill. It's like that friend who always says, "Let's do it!" when you suggest something wild. When dopamine levels are out of whack, it can even contribute to addiction, as the pursuit of that dopamine high overrides better judgment.

But what happens when dopamine levels are low? You might find yourself feeling like you're wading through molasses. Symptoms of dopamine deficiency can include fatigue, lack of motivation, and even depression. It's as if life's color has dulled, leaving you feeling disconnected and unenthused. Conditions such as Parkinson's disease and anhedonia, where pleasure from usually enjoyable activities is absent, are linked to low dopamine levels, highlighting its importance in our daily functioning.

Thankfully, you don't have to accept low dopamine levels as your fate. There are natural ways to give your dopamine a well-deserved boost. Start with regular exercise, which is like a natural dopamine pump. Whether it's a brisk walk, a dance class, or a session at the gym, physical activity increases dopamine production, lifting your mood and energy levels. Dietary choices also play a part. Foods rich in tyrosine, an amino acid precursor to dopamine, can help. Think almonds, dairy, beans, whole grains, and protein-rich foods like beef, chicken, fish, and pork. They're like little packages of dopamine potential, ready to support your brain's reward system.

Engaging in rewarding activities and hobbies is another effective strategy. Whether it's painting, playing an instrument, or gardening, doing what you love stimulates dopamine release. These activities act as mini-rewards, encouraging you to pursue more of what makes you happy. It's like giving your brain a series of small, joyful gifts. By understanding dopamine's role and making these lifestyle tweaks, you can harness its power to enhance your motivation, mood, and overall well-being.

Reflection Section: Boost Your Dopamine Naturally

- Activity Brainstorm: Write down three activities or hobbies that bring you joy. Plan to incorporate them into your week and observe how they influence your mood and motivation.

By embracing the pleasure principle and nurturing your dopamine levels, you can create a life filled with more joy, energy, and satisfaction.

THE MOOD MAESTRO: SEROTONIN'S ROLE IN WELL-BEING

Imagine you're at a party. The music is just right, the snacks are tasty, and everyone's chatting away, feeling pretty good. Picture serotonin as the ultimate party host, ensuring everything runs smoothly and everyone stays happy. This neurotransmitter is a key player in stabilizing mood and fostering feelings of well-being and happiness. Serotonin's influence extends through the serotonergic (seh-ruh-tow-nur-juhk) pathways in the brain, a complex network that's all about keeping your mood in check. It acts like a thermostat, preventing your emotions from getting too hot or too cold and making sure you maintain a comfortable emotional climate. When serotonin levels are balanced, you're more likely to experience a sense of calm and contentment. However, when they're low, it can contribute to mood disorders like depression and anxiety, casting a shadow over even the sunniest days.

Serotonin does more than boost your mood; it also plays a key role in social behavior and how we connect with others. Think of it as the social glue that helps you maintain connections with others. Serotonin influences empathy and social bonding, encouraging you to feel connected and understood by those around you. It's like having an invisible thread linking you to your friends and family. High serotonin levels can enhance these connections, making interactions feel more fulfilling. On the flip side, serotonin also helps regulate aggression and impulse control, acting as a buffer that keeps you from snatching the last cookie at a group gathering. When serotonin is out of balance, these social functions can suffer, leading to increased irritability and decreased patience, which can strain relationships.

Imbalances in serotonin can lead to a range of health issues, impacting both mental and physical well-being. When serotonin levels dip, you might experience symptoms like low mood, irritability, and even sleep disturbances. It's as if life's volume dial has been turned down, leaving you feeling out of tune with the world. Beyond mood, low serotonin is linked to conditions such as obsessive-compulsive disorder (OCD) and irritable bowel syndrome (IBS). In OCD, low serotonin can contribute to repetitive thoughts and behaviors, while in IBS, it can impact gut motility (the movement of food through the digestive tract) and sensitivity, making life a bit more uncomfortable than it should be.

Fortunately, there are practical ways to boost serotonin levels and improve your overall well-being naturally. Start by soaking up some sunlight. Exposure to natural light can increase serotonin synthesis, giving you a mood boost that's as refreshing as a brisk walk in the park. Spending time outdoors, even on a cloudy day, can help your body produce more serotonin, lifting your spirits and energizing your day.

The diet also plays a crucial role in serotonin production. Foods high in tryptophan, an amino acid precursor to serotonin, can help support its synthesis. Think turkey, bananas, and even oats— these foods act like serotonin's best friends, providing the building blocks needed to keep your mood stable. Incorporating these into your meals can help maintain balanced serotonin levels, much like adding a pinch of salt to bring out the flavors in a dish.

Mindfulness meditation is another powerful tool for enhancing serotonin. This practice involves focusing on the present moment, letting go of stress and anxiety, and allowing serotonin to flow more freely. Mindfulness can increase serotonin production, offering a sense of peace and relaxation. Whether it's through guided meditation, yoga, or simply sitting quietly and focusing on your breath, incorporating mindfulness into your daily routine can be a game-changer for your mental health.

THE LOVE BUZZ: OXYTOCIN'S ROLE IN BONDING AND BLISS

Imagine a world where trust and love are tangible, where every hug and shared laughter strengthens bonds like super glue. Enter oxytocin, often called the "love hormone," plays a powerful role in social bonding and intimacy. Picture this: during childbirth, as a mother holds her newborn for the first time, oxytocin floods her system, fostering an unbreakable connection. It's also at work when a mother breastfeeds, creating a nurturing bond that feels as natural as breathing. This hormone isn't just for parents and babies, though. It's the invisible thread weaving through romantic relationships, allowing partners to trust and feel close to each other. Whether it's a gentle touch or a shared smile, oxytocin strengthens these connections, turning everyday moments into something profound.

Beyond the heartwarming family moments, oxytocin also wields its magic on our emotional and psychological states. It's like that calming friend who always knows the right thing to say. By reducing stress and anxiety, oxytocin helps create a sense of calm and stability. It's no surprise, then, that researchers are exploring its therapeutic potential for social phobias and autism. Imagine oxytocin as a gentle coach, guiding individuals to feel more comfortable in social situations and fostering confidence and ease. This hormone's ability to modulate emotional responses makes it a promising candidate for therapies aimed at enhancing social interactions and reducing anxiety.

But oxytocin's benefits aren't confined to the emotional realm. It extends its reach into physical health, offering perks that go beyond warm fuzzy feelings. For starters, oxytocin has been linked to cardiovascular health. It's like a personal trainer for your heart, helping to lower blood pressure and reduce stress-induced damage. Picture it as a soothing balm, counteracting the effects of stress and promoting heart health. Oxytocin also plays a part in wound healing, acting as a nurse speeding up recovery and promoting tissue repair. And let's not forget its role in immune system modulation, bolstering your body's defenses like a vigilant bodyguard. These broader health benefits highlight oxytocin's versatility and importance in maintaining overall well-being.

So, how can you naturally boost your oxytocin levels and enjoy these wide-ranging benefits? Start with the power of touch. Physical contact, whether it's a hug, a pat on the back, or holding hands, can trigger oxytocin release, deepening bonds and enhancing feelings of closeness. Think of it as a mini oxytocin boost, free and readily available. Activities that foster emotional closeness, like sharing experiences or engaging in active listening, also work wonders. Whether it's a shared adventure or a heartfelt conversation, these moments create a fertile ground for oxytocin to flourish. And don't underestimate the power of our furry friends. Petting a dog or cat can significantly increase oxytocin levels, reinforcing the bond between humans and animals. It's like having a little oxytocin generator on four legs, ready to offer companionship and comfort.

As we wrap up our exploration of oxytocin, it's clear that this hormone is a keystone of social and emotional health, weaving its influence through our relationships and our bodies. Whether it's strengthening bonds, reducing stress, or supporting physical health, oxytocin is a multifaceted ally. By understanding its role and incorporating simple practices to boost its levels, you can enhance your emotional connections and overall well-being. This understanding leads naturally to our next discussion, where we will explore hormonal changes across life stages, including puberty, pregnancy, and menopause, and how they shape our experiences and health.

CHAPTER 9
HORMONAL CHANGES ACROSS LIFE STAGES

Have you ever been around a teenager and thought, "Wow, that's a lot of drama for one room"? Maybe you've even been there yourself, riding adolescence's emotional rollercoaster. It's not all slamming doors and mysterious odors, though. There's a lot more happening under the surface, and it all starts with the fascinating world of puberty. This stage of life is like a hormonal fireworks show, where the hypothalamic-pituitary-gonadal (HPG) axis takes center stage, throwing a grand opening party for adulthood.

Let's pause a moment and briefly overview the HPG. The Hypothalamic-pituitary-gonadal (HPG) is a system of endocrine glands that regulates reproduction and associated behaviors in vertebrates (vur-tuh-bruhts). The HPG axis is made up of the hypothalamus, anterior pituitary gland, and gonads (ovaries or testes):

Now, let's not confuse vertebrates with vertebrae. Vertebrates are a category of animals, including humans, that have a backbone and a skeleton. Vertebrae are made of bone and cartilage that make up your spine. The glossary has a more in-depth definition. Alright, we cleared that up, so let's get back to the program.

This axis is the body's way of saying, "It's go time!" by releasing gonadotropin (gow-na-duh-trow-pn) releasing hormone (GnRH). This, in turn, prompts the pituitary gland to produce hormones like luteinizing hormone (LH) and follicle-stimulating hormone (FSH), which then give the ovaries and testes a nudge, telling them to start producing sex hormones like estrogen and testosterone. It's like a chain reaction of hormonal text messages, and the body is the group chat.

As these sex hormones surge, they trigger a variety of physical transformations that are as exciting as they are bewildering. Adolescents experience growth spurts that seem to defy logic. One day, you're looking down at your child, and the next, you're asking them to grab things from the top shelf. These growth spurts are driven by the interaction of sex steroids, growth hormone, and insulin-like growth factor 1 (IGF-1), resulting in the rapid bone growth and maturation that seems to happen overnight . But that's not all—secondary sexual characteristics also make their grand debut. For girls, this means breast development and the onset of menstruation, while boys experience voice deepening and increased muscle mass. It's like Mother Nature decided to throw a surprise puberty party, and everyone's invited.

Alongside these physical changes, puberty also ushers in a whirlwind of emotional and psychological effects. Hormonal fluctuations can lead to increased emotional sensitivity, leaving teenagers feeling everything a bit more intensely. It's common for teens to oscillate between euphoria and despair at the drop of a hat, all thanks to those pesky hormones. Risk-taking behavior is another hallmark of adolescence, with hormones like testosterone fueling a desire for adventure and novelty. This is why your teenage self might have thought climbing the tallest tree or dyeing your hair neon pink was a stellar idea. These behaviors are part of the brain's natural development, as the prefrontal cortex, the part of the brain responsible for decision-making and impulse control, is still under construction and not fully developed until the mid-20s.

Supporting healthy puberty involves a mix of lifestyle and environmental factors. A balanced diet and regular physical activity are crucial for adolescents navigating this transformative period. Proper nutrition supports growth and development, while physical activity helps manage stress and improve mood. Encourage your teens to embrace a variety of foods, including fruits, vegetables, lean proteins, and whole grains, to provide them with the nutrients they need. Meanwhile, staying active—whether through sports, dancing, or even just walking the dog—can help keep those hormones in check.

Open communication and parental support are not just important, they are vital in helping adolescents manage the challenges of puberty. By establishing an open, supportive environment, you can confidently guide your teen through the ups and downs of this stage. Talking about the changes they're going through can help clarify the process, making it feel less overwhelming. Remember, you're not just raising a child; you're guiding a future adult through one of the most significant transitions of their life. Your role in this journey is crucial, and your open communication can empower your teen to face these changes with confidence.

PREGNANCY AND POSTPARTUM: HORMONAL SHIFTS EXPLAINED

Pregnancy is a time when your body embarks on a miraculous journey of transformation. It's as if every cell is whispering, "Let's try something new!" At the heart of this grand transformation is a cocktail of hormones designed to support both you and the developing baby. It all starts with human chorionic gonadotropin (hCG), the hormone responsible for the plus sign on your pregnancy test. hCG levels rise rapidly in early pregnancy, signaling your body to maintain the uterine lining and support the growing fetus. It's like a tiny cheerleader, ensuring everything stays on track for the months ahead. But hCG is just the opening act. As pregnancy progresses, progesterone and estrogen step into the spotlight, driving the changes in your body that prepare you for motherhood. Progesterone keeps the uterine environment snug and nurturing, while estrogen supports fetal development and prepares your body for labor. It's a dynamic duo orchestrating an array of physiological changes that, while miraculous, can sometimes feel like a wild ride.

These hormonal shifts have profound effects on the mother's body and mind. You might find yourself experiencing morning sickness, that delightful feeling of nausea that often hits first thing in the morning (or, let's be honest, whenever it feels like it). This queasiness is linked to rising hCG levels, and while it's a good sign that hormones are doing their job, it doesn't make the bathroom any more inviting. As pregnancy progresses, mood swings can become your new normal. One minute, you're laughing at a cute puppy video, and the next, you're sobbing because someone finished the last pickle. These emotional ups and downs are the result of fluctuating hormones like estrogen and progesterone, which can affect neurotransmitters in your brain. These neurotransmitters, such as serotonin and dopamine, play a key role in regulating mood and can be influenced by hormonal changes, leading to emotional variability. It's like having a theater troupe perform a different play every day, with your emotions in the starring role.

Once the baby makes their grand entrance, your hormones decide to shake things up again, leading to postpartum hormonal adjustments that can feel like you're on a hormonal rollercoaster. After childbirth, there's a sharp drop in progesterone and estrogen, which can leave you feeling like your emotional safety net has been pulled out from under you. It's a time when the body is recalibrating, and the sudden hormonal shifts can contribute to the baby blues or even postpartum depression. Prolactin, the hormone responsible for milk production, becomes the star player as it facilitates breastfeeding and helps bond with your newborn. It's a time of incredible change, both physically and emotionally, as your body recovers from pregnancy and adjusts to its new role.

Managing these postpartum changes requires a blend of rest, nutrition, and support. Prioritizing rest is crucial, even though sleep might feel like a distant memory. Grab naps when you can, and remember that it's okay if the laundry piles up. Proper nutrition is another key factor, helping to replenish your body's stores and support recovery. Focus on nutrient-rich foods like lean proteins, fruits, and vegetables, and don't shy away from healthy fats that provide the energy you need. Seeking social support and professional help is also vital. Whether it's a trusted friend, a family member, or a mental health professional, having a support system can be incredibly beneficial. Talking about your feelings and experiences can lighten the burden of postpartum challenges, offering reassurance that you're not alone in this journey.

MENOPAUSE AND ANDROPAUSE: UNDERSTANDING THE TRANSITION

Ah, menopause. It's the time in life when your body decides it's had enough of the monthly subscription service you never signed up for. This transition is characterized by a notable decrease in estrogen and progesterone levels, resulting in the end of menstrual cycles. Think of it as your body's way of saying, "We're closing up shop." For many women, this hormonal shift can feel like stepping into uncharted territory. It's not just about the end of periods; it's about navigating a new phase with a cocktail of symptoms and health considerations. Hot flashes and night sweats often steal the spotlight, catching you off guard in the middle of a meeting or during a peaceful night's sleep. They're like your body's way of reminding you it's still in charge. But the drama doesn't end there. Menopause also increases the risk of osteoporosis and cardiovascular disease as the protective effects of estrogen wane. It's like the body's bouncer has quit, leaving the gates open for these conditions to sneak in.

While menopause has its well-publicized symptoms, andropause, or the so-called "male menopause," tends to fly under the radar. This phase involves a gradual decline in testosterone levels in middle-aged men. Unlike the abrupt changes women experience, andropause is more like a slow fade-out. It's not a universal experience—some men breeze through midlife without a hitch, but others may notice a dip in energy, mood changes, and shifts in sexual health. It's as if the body's engine is still running but needs more tune-ups to maintain its former performance. The decline in testosterone can lead to fatigue, reduced muscle mass, and a decrease in libido, making it feel like the zest for life has simmered down a bit. But fear not because navigating these changes doesn't mean resigning yourself to anything less than a vibrant life.

Supporting healthy aging through menopause and andropause involves a mix of lifestyle tweaks and, sometimes, medical interventions. Hormone replacement therapy (HRT) is one option that can help alleviate the symptoms of menopause and andropause by supplementing declining hormone levels. It's like giving your body a little boost to keep things running smoothly. However, HRT isn't for everyone, and it's important to weigh the benefits and risks with a healthcare provider. Alongside HRT, maintaining a healthy diet and engaging in regular exercise are key. A diet rich in calcium and vitamin D supports bone health, while regular physical activity helps maintain muscle mass, boost mood, and manage weight. It's like giving your body the tools it needs to keep on trucking.

Stress reduction and mental health strategies are also vital components of aging gracefully. Techniques such as mindfulness, meditation, and yoga can help manage stress and improve emotional well-being. They're like your body's version of a spa day, offering relaxation and rejuvenation when you need it most. These practices not only help keep stress hormones like cortisol in check but also foster a positive outlook, which is essential for navigating the changes that come with age. Remember, embracing these strategies isn't just about managing symptoms—it's about enhancing your quality of life and staying active, engaged, and vibrant as you move through these natural stages.

As we wrap up this chapter on hormonal transitions, it's clear that understanding and embracing these changes can empower you to live your best life at any age. By taking proactive steps toward health and well-being, you can sail through menopause and androstenedione with confidence and vitality. Up next, we'll explore how diet, nutrition, and lifestyle choices can further support hormonal health, providing you with practical tools to balance your hormones naturally.

CHAPTER 10

DIET, NUTRITION, AND HORMONAL HEALTH

Imagine standing in front of your fridge, pondering why some days you feel invincible and others, well, not so much. The answer could be in your diet. But fear not, you're about to embark on a journey of understanding and empowerment. Welcome to the world of clean eating, where your diet can be your greatest ally in achieving hormonal harmony. Clean eating, a return to basics, is about embracing whole, unprocessed foods that would make your grandparents proud. Think fresh fruits and vegetables, whole grains, legumes, lean proteins, and healthy fats as the stars of your plate, all playing a crucial role in maintaining hormonal balance.

Let's break it down. Fresh fruits and vegetables are your body's best friends. They are loaded with vitamins, minerals, and antioxidants that aid your body's natural detoxification processes, helping to flush out those pesky hormone disruptors that sneak in through processed foods and environmental factors. Whole grains and legumes, like oats and lentils, provide a steady energy source, keeping your blood sugar levels stable and preventing those hangry moments. Lean proteins, such as chicken and fish, are essential for maintaining muscle mass and producing hormones, while healthy fats, like those found in avocados and olive oil, support brain health and hormone production. Together, these foods create a balanced, nutrient-dense diet that promotes hormonal balance and improves overall health.

Clean eating offers a myriad of benefits for hormonal health. Keeping blood sugar levels steady helps prevent insulin spikes that can trigger mood swings, energy crashes, and potential weight gain. Research from the Marion Gluck Clinic shows that nutrients from whole foods aid in hormone production, metabolism, and detoxification, giving your body the essential tools to function at its best. Clean eating also reduces inflammation, a known contributor to hormonal imbalances. By eliminating processed foods and focusing on whole, natural ingredients, you create an anti-inflammatory environment in your body that can help reduce symptoms like bloating, fatigue, and skin problems.

Transitioning to a clean eating lifestyle might sound daunting at first, but rest assured, it's simpler than you think. Start by planning your meals around whole foods. Instead of grabbing a pre-packaged meal, think about how you can incorporate more fresh produce into your day. Maybe swap that sugary cereal for a bowl of oatmeal topped with berries and nuts. When grocery shopping, take the time to read labels. Look for products with minimal ingredients and avoid additives and preservatives that can disrupt your hormones. Think of it as being a food detective, sleuthing out the sneaky culprits hiding in your snacks. This simple approach will make the transition to clean eating feel more manageable and less overwhelming.

Of course, every new habit comes with its challenges. You might find yourself pressed for time when it comes to meal preparation. To tackle this, consider setting aside a few hours each week for meal prep. Cook in batches, chop your veggies in advance, and store everything in easy-to-grab containers. This way, you'll always have a healthy option at your fingertips, even on your busiest days. Cravings for processed foods can also be a hurdle. If you find yourself yearning for that bag of chips, try reaching for a handful of nuts or a piece of fruit instead. These healthy swaps can satisfy your cravings while keeping your hormones happy.

Meal Planning: Outline a week's worth of meals centered around whole foods, incorporating a mix of textures and colors to make each meal both tasty and interesting. Consider any challenges that arise and think of ways to keep your plan on track. This forward-thinking approach supports healthy eating, saves time, and reduces stress throughout the week. Embracing clean eating is a powerful, proactive step toward well-being, and meal planning is a key tool in this journey.

Take a step toward balancing your hormones and enhancing your overall health. Remember, it's about progress, not perfection. Each small change you make can have a big impact on your well-being, helping you feel more energized, balanced, and ready to tackle whatever life throws your way. And the best part? Clean eating is not a rigid set of rules but a flexible approach that you can adapt to your lifestyle and preferences, making it a liberating and empowering choice. This flexibility allows you to make choices that suit your individual needs and preferences, giving you a sense of control over your health journey.

SUPERFOODS FOR HORMONAL SUPPORT

Imagine your kitchen as a superhero headquarters, with a lineup of superfoods ready to help you tackle hormonal imbalances. These superfoods are like the caped crusaders of nutrition, each offering unique benefits to support your body's intricate hormonal web. Take flaxseeds, for instance. These tiny seeds are packed with lignans, compounds that can help balance estrogen levels in the body. By mimicking estrogen in a gentle way, lignans can modulate estrogen activity, making them especially beneficial for those experiencing symptoms of estrogen dominance. Flaxseeds can be easily sprinkled on your morning oatmeal or added to smoothies, making them a versatile addition to your diet. Here is a short list of superfoods to consider adding to your diet;

- Avocados
- Berries
- Cruciferous vegetables like broccoli, cauliflower, kale, spinach
- Nuts
- Salmon for the omega-fatty acids, or consider taking a fish oil supplement
- Quality protein
- Pre-biotic and probiotics

Now, let's talk about the mighty maca root. Known for its energizing properties, maca is often touted as a natural booster for energy, stamina, and libido. This root has been used for centuries in traditional medicine, particularly in the Andes, where it grows. Maca is thought to support hormonal health by nourishing the endocrine system, which is responsible for hormone production. Incorporating maca into your routine is as easy as adding a spoonful of maca powder to your morning smoothie or mixing it into baked goods for a subtle, nutty flavor.

Dark leafy greens are another powerhouse of hormonal support. These greens, including kale, spinach, and Swiss chard, are rich in nutrients that promote detoxification and support liver function. The liver is a key player in hormone metabolism, helping to process and eliminate excess hormones from the body. By aiding in detoxification, dark leafy greens can help maintain hormonal balance and reduce symptoms of imbalance. You can enjoy these greens in a variety of ways, from tossing them into a salad, blending them into a smoothie, or sautéing them as a side dish.

The nutrient profiles of these superfoods offer specific benefits that can help balance hormones and improve overall health. For instance, chia seeds, another superfood, are rich in omega-3 fatty acids, known for their anti-inflammatory effects. Omega-3s can help reduce inflammation-related hormonal imbalances, which are often at the root of conditions like PMS and menopause symptoms.

Antioxidants found in berries, such as blueberries and strawberries, combat oxidative stress, protect your cells from damage, and support a healthy hormonal environment. These antioxidants can help mitigate the effects of stress on your hormones, making berries a sweet and beneficial treat.

Adding superfoods to your daily meals and snacks can be easy and enjoyable. Smoothies are a great way to combine several superfoods into one tasty drink. Try blending spinach, berries, flaxseeds, and a scoop of maca powder with your favorite milk for a nutrient-packed breakfast or snack. Superfood salads and bowls are another easy option. Start with a base of dark leafy greens, add a variety of colorful vegetables, and top with seeds, nuts, and a drizzle of olive oil. For snacks, keep it simple with a handful of nuts and seeds or a small bowl of berries and apple slices.

While superfoods offer incredible benefits, it's important to be mindful of any potential limitations. For instance, although cruciferous vegetables are highly nutritious, they may not be ideal for those with thyroid issues. These vegetables can interfere with thyroid function if consumed in large quantities, so it's wise to moderate your intake if you have thyroid concerns. Additionally, some people may have allergies to certain superfoods, like nuts, which can cause adverse reactions. It's always a good idea to listen to your body and consult with a healthcare provider if you're uncertain about incorporating a particular superfood into your diet.

THE IMPACT OF SUGAR AND PROCESSED FOODS ON HORMONES

Imagine this: you're at a party, surrounded by a table full of sweets that could make even Willy Wonka jealous. You indulge in a few cupcakes, some chocolate, and maybe a cookie or two. But then, the sugar crash hits, and suddenly, you're not feeling so sweet. Ever wondered why that is? Sugar has a sneaky way of wreaking havoc on your hormones, much like an uninvited guest at a party. When you consume excessive sugar, your body releases more insulin to manage the sugar levels in your blood. Over time, this can lead to insulin resistance, where your cells become less responsive to insulin's instructions. It's like your body's trying to have a conversation, but the cells just aren't listening. This resistance can lead to a whole host of problems, including weight gain, fatigue, and an increased risk of type 2 diabetes.

But that's not all. Sugar spikes can also lead to an increase in cortisol production. You might remember cortisol as the "stress hormone," when it's released in excess, it can leave you feeling jittery and anxious like you've had too many cups of coffee. This can create a vicious cycle of stress and fatigue, leaving you feeling more stressed and tired than before you indulged in those sweets. It's as if sugar is playing a cruel game, promising a moment of bliss only to leave you with a sugar-fueled rollercoaster of emotions.

Let's not forget about processed foods, those convenient yet often unhealthy options lurking in our pantries. Processed foods are typically packed with additives and preservatives that can disrupt your hormonal balance. Artificial sweeteners, for instance, might seem like a harmless alternative to sugar, but they can interfere with your body's endocrine system, which regulates hormone production. It's like throwing a wrench into a well-oiled machine, causing it to malfunction. Trans fats, commonly present in processed foods, can interfere with estrogen levels, potentially causing hormonal imbalances that impact mood and energy.

So, how can you reduce sugar and processed foods in your diet? Start by identifying hidden sugars on food labels. These sneaky sugars often hide under names like high fructose corn syrup or sucrose, so keep an eye out. Cooking at home using whole ingredients is another great strategy, allowing you to control what goes into your meals. Think of it as taking back control of the kitchen, one meal at a time. Gradually reducing sugary beverages, like sodas and energy drinks, can also make a big difference. Swap your can of soda for a glass of water infused with fresh fruit, and you'll be surprised at how your energy levels stabilize.

Natural sweeteners and whole food options are your allies in this quest for better health. Natural sweeteners like honey or stevia offer the sweetness you crave without causing the sharp sugar highs and lows. They're like the friendlier, more balanced alternatives to refined sugar. Whole foods, such as fresh fruits, offer natural sweetness and are packed with vitamins, minerals, and fiber that support overall health. When you need a sweet fix, reach for an apple or a handful of berries instead of processed snacks.

Remember that moderation is key as we wrap up our exploration of sugar's impact on hormones. By making mindful choices and embracing whole foods, you can create a diet that supports hormonal balance and overall well-being. With a little effort, you can keep those pesky sugar crashes at bay and enjoy more stable energy levels throughout the day. In the next chapter, we'll explore how to integrate Eastern and Western practices for a holistic approach to hormonal health.

CHAPTER 11
INTEGRATING EASTERN AND WESTERN PRACTICES

Imagine your body as a bustling city, with hormones as the city's workers, tirelessly keeping everything running smoothly. Now, picture Ayurveda as the wise city planner, ensuring every worker is where they need to be, all while maintaining balance and harmony throughout the city. This ancient Indian system of medicine offers a holistic approach to health, emphasizing the interconnectedness of the mind, body, and spirit. Ayurveda, which means "the science of life," is about achieving balance and promoting well-being by understanding your unique constitution, or Prakriti, which combines the three doshas: Vata, Pitta, and Kapha. Each of us has a unique blend of these doshas, like a personalized cocktail that influences our physical, mental, and emotional traits.

What is a dosha, you ask? Well, my friend, Ayurveda is an ancient Indian medical system based on ancient writings that rely on a natural and holistic approach to physical and mental health. Doshas are a part of Ayurveda and have three categories of substances that are thought to be present in a person's mind and body.

The three doshas play a significant role in determining how we respond to the world around us. Vata, associated with air and space, governs movement and communication, making it the social butterfly of the doshas. Pitta, linked to fire and water, is all about transformation and is responsible for digestion and metabolism—think of it as the passionate and fiery go-getter. Kapha, aligned with earth and water, offers stability and structure, acting as the calming force that keeps everything grounded. Just like a good recipe requires the right balance of ingredients, maintaining harmony among the doshas is key to optimal health. Imbalances in the doshas can lead to various health issues, including hormonal imbalances that can throw your body's rhythm off-key faster than a karaoke night gone wrong.

Ayurveda offers an array of remedies to support hormonal health, focusing on natural treatments that address both symptoms and root causes. Ashwagandha, a powerful adaptogenic herb, is well-known for its ability to reduce stress and manage cortisol levels. It's like a calming cup of tea for your adrenal glands, helping to soothe the effects of chronic stress and keep cortisol in check. Shatavari (also called Asparagus racemosus), often referred to as a woman's best friend, supports female reproductive health by nourishing the reproductive system and balancing hormones. It's particularly beneficial for women experiencing menstrual irregularities or menopausal symptoms. Triphala, a blend of three fruits, is a go-to for detoxification and digestive health, promoting regularity and cleansing the body of toxins. Together, these Ayurvedic herbs create a powerful trinity to support hormonal balance and overall wellness.

In Ayurveda, diet and lifestyle are as crucial as the remedies themselves. Seasonal eating, for instance, encourages you to align your diet with the earth's natural rhythms, choosing foods that balance the doshas according to the time of year. Eating warm, cooked foods in winter can help balance Vata, while lighter, cooling foods in summer can pacify Pitta. Daily routines, or Dinacharya, are another cornerstone of Ayurvedic practice. Dinacharya is a set of daily self-care practices that are designed to align your body with the natural rhythms of the day. By establishing regular habits, such as waking up early, practicing self-care, and eating meals at consistent times, you create a sense of stability that supports hormonal harmony. Incorporating meditation and yoga into your routine can further enhance balance, calming the mind and reducing stress. These practices promote mindfulness and help maintain the delicate equilibrium of your doshas.

Reflection Section: Ayurveda in Action

- Journaling Prompt: Reflect on your current daily routine. Are there areas where you can incorporate Ayurvedic practices, such as seasonal eating or establishing a Dinacharya? Jot down a plan to introduce one new practice over the next week and observe any changes in how you feel.

Ayurveda and TCM, with their holistic approaches, have been instrumental in transforming the lives of many individuals struggling with hormonal imbalances. These systems of medicine understand that each person is unique, with their own set of challenges and needs. Take Sarah, for instance, who battled irregular menstrual cycles and stress-related exhaustion. By incorporating Ashwagandha into her routine and embracing daily yoga practices, Sarah found relief from her symptoms and regained her energy. Then there's John, who grappled with digestive issues and mood swings. With the help of Triphala and a tailored Ayurvedic diet, John experienced improved digestion and a renewed sense of balance. These stories of transformation underscore the individualized and catered nature of Ayurveda and TCM in addressing hormonal health.

TRADITIONAL CHINESE MEDICINE: A HOLISTIC APPROACH

If you've ever felt out of balance, like your body's internal playlist got stuck on shuffle, then Traditional Chinese Medicine (TCM) might just be your jam. TCM is all about harmony—picture Yin and Yang as the ultimate cosmic dance partners, each with their own unique moves. In TCM, health is achieved when there's a balance between these forces, with Yin representing the cool, calm, and collected, and Yang bringing the heat and energy. The Five Elements theory—wood, fire, earth, metal, and water—also plays a role, each element representing different organs and emotions. It's like your body's internal council meeting, where everything needs to be in sync for optimal health. Then there's Qi, the life force energy that flows through meridians, or pathways, in the body. When Qi is disrupted, it's like a traffic jam on the highway of your health, leading to all sorts of hormonal hiccups. But don't worry; TCM has plenty of tools to help clear the roadblocks and restore balance, leaving you feeling reassured and at peace.

But don't worry; TCM has plenty of tools to help clear the roadblocks. Acupuncture, for instance, might sound like a strange way to spend an afternoon—who willingly turns themselves into a human pincushion? Yet, it's been shown to effectively regulate menstrual cycles by restoring the flow of Qi and balancing hormones. It's like hitting the reset button on your body's control panel. Herbal formulas also hold a special place in TCM, with Dong Quai often dubbed the "female ginseng" for its ability to support hormonal health. This herb is a powerhouse for those dealing with menstrual irregularities and menopausal symptoms. And let's not forget moxibustion, a practice that involves burning dried mugwort near the skin to warm and invigorate the flow of Qi. It's like a cozy campfire for your energy pathways, providing warmth and balance.

When it comes to diet, TCM offers some deliciously warming advice. Foods are categorized by their energetic properties, and warming foods are often recommended to balance Yin and Yang. Imagine sipping on a bowl of ginger chicken soup on a cold day— it's not just comforting; it's helping to balance your internal thermostat. TCM also places a strong emphasis on strengthening the liver and kidneys, organs crucial for maintaining hormonal balance. Foods like black beans, walnuts, and goji berries are staples, offering support to these vital organs. Think of them as your body's own personal trainers, keeping everything in top shape.

Research and anecdotal evidence continue to spotlight TCM's potential. Studies have shown acupuncture's positive impact on stress hormones, often resulting in improved mood and reduced anxiety. It's like getting a massage for your mind and body, helping you feel more centered and calm. Many individuals report improved hormonal balance through TCM after years of struggling with conventional treatments. Take Emily, for example, who found relief from her irregular cycles through a combination of acupuncture and herbal formulas. Or David, who turned to TCM for support with stress and energy levels, only to discover a newfound vitality that he hadn't felt in years. These personal stories highlight how TCM can offer a different perspective and complement other approaches to health.

BRIDGING THE GAP: INTEGRATING MODERN MEDICINE

Finding the sweet spot between modern medicine and Eastern practices can feel like trying to balance a spoon on your nose—it takes finesse, but once achieved, it can be gratifying. Integrating these approaches offers a holistic strategy for hormonal health, marrying the best of both worlds. Imagine using the precision of Western diagnostic tools, such as blood tests, to pinpoint exactly what's going on with your hormones. These tests give you a detailed snapshot, much like a high-definition photo of your internal workings, revealing what hormones might be out of whack. Pair this with Eastern practices, which offer a broader view of your body's balance and energy flow, and you've got a more complete picture. It's like having a map and a compass on your health adventure.

Combining pharmaceutical interventions with herbal remedies can create a powerful synergy. Modern medicine excels in offering fast-acting solutions to acute issues—think of it as the superhero that swoops in to save the day. Meanwhile, Eastern practices provide ongoing support, gently nudging your body back into balance over time. For instance, a prescribed medication might swiftly address a hormonal imbalance, while an herbal remedy, such as ginseng, can reinforce the body's natural equilibrium. This approach requires open-minded practitioners who appreciate the strengths of each system. It's not about choosing one over the other but finding a harmonious blend that works for you.

Creating individualized treatment plans that incorporate both Eastern and Western modalities is like customizing a playlist to suit your mood. Collaborative care models are essential, involving practitioners from both traditions who work together to tailor treatments to your specific needs. This collaboration can lead to more personalized care, reflecting your cultural background, beliefs, and preferences. Whether you're more comfortable with acupuncture needles or prefer the familiarity of a pharmacy pill bottle, your treatment plan should respect your choices and enhance your comfort level. Personalization is key, and having a team that respects and understands this can make all the difference.

Evidence-based practice is at the heart of successful integration. It's crucial to ensure that treatments are not only holistic but also safe and effective. Clinical trials on herbal supplements, for example, can provide valuable insights into how these natural remedies interact with conventional medications. Research on lifestyle interventions supported by both traditions offers a solid foundation for combining practices. This evidence serves as a guide, helping practitioners make informed decisions about which treatments to recommend. It's like having a recipe book filled with tried-and-true dishes, ensuring you're serving up the best possible options for your health.

However, integrating these practices isn't without its challenges. Navigating potential interactions between herbs and medications requires careful consideration. Just as you wouldn't mix certain foods that don't go well together, it's essential to understand how different treatments might interact. This is where communication with healthcare providers becomes critical. Open conversations about what you're taking—whether it's a prescription or a herbal supplement—can help prevent any unwanted side effects. Cultural sensitivity and patient education are equally important. Ensuring that patients understand the rationale behind their treatment choices empowers them to take an active role in their health. It's all about creating a dialogue, not a monologue, where patients and practitioners work together as a team.

As we wrap up our chat on blending Eastern and Western medicine, it's clear that this integrative approach offers a comprehensive strategy for hormonal health. By combining the precision and innovation of modern medicine with the wisdom and balance of Eastern practices, you can create a personalized health plan that supports your well-being. This chapter sets the stage for exploring how lifestyle changes can further enhance your hormonal health, leading us into the next chapter with a sense of curiosity and anticipation.

CHAPTER 12
NATURAL REMEDIES AND LIFESTYLE ADJUSTMENTS

Have you ever noticed how some people breeze through life's stressors, like swatting away pesky flies while the tiniest hiccup bogs down others? It's like some folks have an invisible armor against stress, leaving the rest of us wondering if we're missing out on a secret shield. Meet adaptogens, nature's little helpers. These aren't just your average herbs—think of them as the unsung superheroes of the botanical world. Adaptogens are a class of plants, including herbs, roots, and mushrooms, that help balance, restore, and protect the body. They've been used in traditional medicine for centuries, playing roles in Ayurveda and Chinese medicine long before they were trendy. Imagine Rhodiola, a mighty root that can help you power through the daily grind, or holy basil, revered in Ayurvedic medicine for its calming properties. These herbs have stood the test of time, helping humans adapt to stress and maintain balance, much like that friend who always has the perfect advice for every crisis.

At a physiological level, adaptogens are like your body's personal trainers, whipping your stress responses into shape. They function by interacting with the hypothalamic-pituitary-adrenal (HPA) axis, a system that manages stress and regulates hormones such as cortisol. You see when stress hits, the HPA axis coordinates the release of cortisol, that pesky hormone that likes to hang around and wreak havoc on your mood and waistline if left unchecked. Adaptogens help modulate this response, ensuring cortisol levels stay in a healthy range so you don't feel like you're perpetually running from a bear. It's like having a built-in stress thermostat, keeping things cool and balanced even when life gets a bit too hot to handle.

The health benefits of adaptogens extend far beyond stress relief, offering a buffet of perks for your body and mind. They've been shown to improve mental clarity and focus, making them great companions for those marathon study sessions or back-to-back meetings. Imagine sipping on a cup of adaptogen-infused tea and feeling your brain fog clear, like a mist lifting to reveal a sunny day. Not only do they help sharpen your mind, but they also enhance physical endurance and recovery, making them favorites among athletes and gym enthusiasts alike. Adaptogens can give you that extra boost to power through a workout or help your muscles recover faster so you don't feel like a sack of potatoes the next day. They even support immune function, acting like a personal body-guard to fend off those pesky seasonal bugs.

Incorporating adaptogens into your daily life is as easy as pie and just as rewarding. You can enjoy them in teas and tinctures, letting the warm, herbal flavors soothe you as they work their magic. Adding them to smoothies or soups is another delicious way to reap their benefits, turning your meals into nutrient-packed powerhouses. When it comes to dosages, it's best to start small and gradually increase, paying attention to how your body responds. Always check in with a healthcare provider, especially if you're on medication, as some adaptogens can interact with other treatments. Think of it as inviting new friends to a party—you want to ensure everyone gets along before things get wild. As with many things in life, moderation is key. It's often recommended to rotate adaptogens every few months for the best results. This means using a different adaptogen for a period of time before switching to another, as each adaptogen has its unique set of benefits and rotating them can prevent your body from getting used to a particular adaptogen, ensuring you continue to experience their full range of benefits.

Reflection Section: Meet Your Adaptogen Allies

- Adaptogen Diary: Try incorporating one adaptogen into your routine for a week, whether it's a morning rhodiola tea or a pinch of holy basil in your dinner. Note any changes in mood, energy, or stress levels. Consider this your personal experiment in stress management, and remember to enjoy the journey!

Adaptogens are an excellent addition to any lifestyle, providing support and balance in a world that often feels out of control. By understanding and incorporating these natural wonders into your routine, you'll be better equipped to handle whatever life throws your way.

YOGA AND MEDITATION: TOOLS FOR HORMONAL BALANCE

Ever find yourself in the middle of a hectic day, feeling like a tightly wound spring? Yoga might just be the antidote you need. This ancient practice isn't just about contorting into pretzel-like shapes or impressing your friends with a perfect headstand. It's a powerful tool for hormonal health, offering benefits that go far beyond flexibility.

Consistent yoga practice has been found to lower cortisol levels by fostering relaxation and supporting deep, mindful breathing. Yoga serves as a gentle reset for your stress response, helping you navigate life's turbulent moments with a touch more ease. But it doesn't stop there. Yoga can also enhance thyroid function, stimulating this crucial gland to maintain a healthy metabolism and energy balance. It's like giving your thyroid a friendly nudge, whispering, "Hey, let's keep things running smoothly down there."

Certain yoga poses are particularly effective for supporting hormonal health and are easier than you might think. Take the Supported Fish Pose, for instance. This pose gently opens up the throat area, providing a lovely stretch that can help stimulate the thyroid gland. It's a bit like offering your thyroid a spa day, complete with a gentle massage. Then there's Child's Pose, a comforting position that supports the adrenal glands. This pose encourages relaxation and stress relief, making it ideal for those days when you just need a moment to breathe and let the world melt away. And let's not forget the Legs-Up-The-Wall Pose, which is as simple as it sounds. By lying on your back with your legs resting against a wall, you can promote relaxation and circulation, allowing your body to unwind and recalibrate. Each of these poses offers a little calm oasis, helping restore balance in a busy life.

But yoga isn't the only game in town when it comes to calming your hormones. Meditation is another powerful ally, offering a way to cultivate inner peace and hormonal harmony. Mindfulness meditation, in particular, is great for enhancing emotional regulation. It teaches you to observe your thoughts and feelings without judgment, reducing stress and helping you respond to life's challenges with a clear mind. It's like having a mental tidy-up, sweeping away clutter, and creating a calm space. Loving-kindness meditation, on the other hand, focuses on generating feelings of compassion and goodwill for yourself and others. This practice can increase oxytocin levels, the "love hormone" that supports emotional well-being and strengthens social bonds. Think of it as sending a warm, fuzzy hug to your brain, promoting feelings of connection and contentment.

Integrating yoga and meditation into a holistic practice can offer profound benefits for your hormonal health. Establishing a daily routine is a great way to start. Aim for consistency, even if it's just a few minutes each day, to create a sense of rhythm and balance in your life. Consider setting up a calming environment for your practice—a dedicated space with a yoga mat, some soft lighting, and perhaps a bit of soothing music. This sacred space can become your personal retreat, where you can recharge and reconnect. If you're new to meditation or yoga, guided meditations and yoga apps can be incredibly helpful. They offer step-by-step instructions and encouragement, making it easy to get started and stick with it. With these tools in hand, you can nurture a practice that supports your hormonal health and enhances your overall well-being.

BUILDING A HORMONE-FRIENDLY LIFESTYLE

Ever had one of those days where you're so out of sync it feels like you're trying to hit a piñata in complete darkness? Our bodies love routines. Establishing daily habits that align with your natural hormonal rhythms is like giving your body a map with clear directions. It starts with something as simple as keeping a consistent sleep schedule. Your body thrives on predictability. Going to bed and waking up at the same time every day can do wonders for your hormonal health. Think of it as setting your internal alarm clock, gently guiding your body through the cycles of sleep and wakefulness without the rude awakening of a blaring alarm.

Now, let's talk food. Regular meal times aren't just for keeping hunger at bay; they play a crucial role in regulating insulin levels. Skipping meals or eating erratically can send your blood sugar on a rollercoaster ride, leaving you feeling like you've run a marathon when you haven't even left your chair. Aim for balanced meals at regular intervals to keep things steady. Your body will thank you for not crashing in the middle of your mid-morning meeting.

Of course, what you eat matters, too. Environmental and lifestyle factors can sneakily impact your hormonal health. Endocrine-disrupting chemicals (EDCs) are the villains lurking in our environment, found in everything from plastics to pesticides. They can interfere with hormone function, making your body feel like it's operating in a fog. Reducing your exposure to these chemicals is a simple yet powerful step. Opt for organic foods when possible to minimize pesticide intake. Not only will your hormones thank you, but you'll be doing a little happy dance for your overall health.

Exercise also plays a pivotal role in your hormonal balance. Aerobic exercises like walking, running, or cycling are fantastic for reducing stress hormones and enhancing mood. Picture this: a brisk walk can clear your mind and help your body process and reduce cortisol, the notorious stress hormone, making you feel lighter, both physically and mentally. For those looking to boost testosterone, strength training is your go-to. Lifting weights or engaging in resistance exercises not only helps build muscle but also supports healthy hormone production. And don't forget about the gentler forms of exercise, like tai chi or pilates. These can help maintain overall balance, improve flexibility, and reduce stress without the intensity of a high-impact workout.

But another, often overlooked aspect of hormonal health is social connections and emotional well-being. Building supportive relationships and participating in community activities can profoundly affect your hormones. Positive social interactions stimulate the release of oxytocin, that warm-fuzzy hormone that reinforces bonds and promotes feelings of trust and love. Remember, laughter isn't just contagious; it's a powerful stress buster. Sharing a hearty laugh with friends can lower cortisol and elevate mood, making it one of the most enjoyable ways to support hormonal health. So, don't hesitate to reach out to loved ones, join a club, or partake in activities that bring you joy.

In wrapping up this chapter, it's clear that creating a hormone-friendly lifestyle isn't about major life overhauls. Instead, it's about integrating small, deliberate changes that align with your body's natural rhythms. As you continue your journey to understanding hormones, remember that each step towards balance is a step towards a healthier, happier you. Up next, we'll explore how to debunk common hormonal myths, helping you navigate the sea of misinformation with confidence and clarity.

CHAPTER 13

MYTH-BUSTING HORMONAL MISCONCEPTIONS

Have you ever been told you're acting a bit hormonal? It's like someone's accusing you of being possessed by a mysterious force only understood by a select few. Hormones often get a bad rap, as if they're the scapegoats for every emotional outburst and odd craving. But let's face it, these little chemical messengers are as misunderstood as quantum physics at a cocktail party. In this chapter, we will tackle some of the common myths surrounding hormones because, frankly, they deserve a better PR team.

DEBUNKING HORMONAL MYTHS: WHAT SCIENCE SAYS

First up is the notion that hormonal imbalances are a female-only affair. Spoiler alert: they're not. Sure, women have a complex symphony of hormones that orchestrate everything from mood swings to hot flashes, but men aren't just sitting in the audience eating popcorn. Testosterone, the big kahuna in the male hormonal world, can also be a bit of a diva. Low testosterone levels can bring on fatigue, reduced libido, and even weight gain—much like finding out your favorite action hero would rather knit than save the day.. Men can experience irritability and mood changes when testosterone levels aren't playing nice, proving that hormones don't discriminate by gender.

Cortisol, the not-so-silent stress hormone, plays a role across the board. Both men and women can experience elevated cortisol levels due to chronic stress, leading to the not-so-fun party of weight gain, anxiety, and sleep issues. So, next time someone says hormones are just a "women's problem," feel free to enlighten them with some science.

Now, let's address the myth that you can't control your hormones. It's easy to feel like hormones are the puppet masters pulling the strings, but you're not entirely at their mercy. The choices you make in your lifestyle can greatly influence your hormone levels. Regular exercise, for instance, is like giving your hormones a pep talk, encouraging balance, and improving insulin regulation. A balanced diet rich in essential nutrients like zinc and omega-3 fatty acids can support hormone synthesis, creating a harmonious environment for your body's internal workings. And let's not forget stress management. Techniques like meditation or simply taking a walk in nature can help keep cortisol in check, preventing it from running rampant like a toddler on a sugar high.

Speaking of control, let's talk about hormone replacement therapies (HRT). There's a misconception that all hormone therapies are dangerous and best avoided, but that's not entirely true.Hormone replacement therapy (HRT) can be an effective tool for managing symptoms of hormonal imbalances, particularly during menopause. However, not all HRT is created equal.

Bioidentical hormones, which are chemically identical to the hormones produced by your body, offer an alternative to synthetic versions.

FDA-approved bioidentical hormones have undergone safety testing, whereas compounded versions have not been tested to the same extent. While there are risks associated with HRT, recent studies suggest that proper medical supervision can alleviate symptoms like hot flashes and mood swings. It's all about finding the balance that works for you, and that means having an open dialogue with your healthcare provider.

On to natural supplements, which often get the halo effect of being safe simply because they're "natural." But here's the thing: just because something grows in nature doesn't mean it's free of side effects, like poison ivy, for example. Supplements used for hormone health can interact with medications and cause unforeseen reactions. They're not as heavily regulated as pharmaceuticals, leading to variations in quality and potential risks. Before adding a new supplement to your routine, it's wise to consult with a healthcare provider to ensure it doesn't do more harm than good. Just because it's on a shelf at your local health store doesn't mean it's a free-for-all.

Reflection Section: Myth or Fact?

- Quiz Yourself: Think you can separate fact from fiction when it comes to hormones? Test your knowledge with a quick quiz. Are hormonal imbalances exclusive to women? Can lifestyle changes really influence hormone levels? True or false: all hormone therapies are unsafe. Take a moment to jot down your answers and see how many myths you've busted!

Understanding these myths and the truths behind them can empower you to take charge of your hormonal health. Whether it's through informed lifestyle choices, cautious use of natural supplements, or considering HRT with medical guidance, you have more control over your hormones than you might think. So, the next time someone tries to blame hormones for every little hiccup, you'll be armed with the knowledge to set the record straight.

NAVIGATING HORMONAL HEALTH TRUTHS AND LIES

Let's tackle the first truth: stress is a sneaky saboteur of hormonal health. Picture stress as that unwelcome guest who crashes your peaceful party; before you know it, everyone's running around in chaos. Chronic stress, that long-term, relentless type, has a way of throwing your adrenal hormones into a tailspin. When you're stressed, your adrenal glands release cortisol, the hormone that helps you cope with those tense moments. It's great for short bursts, like when you must escape a traffic jam or meet a deadline. But cortisol levels stay elevated when stress becomes a permanent fixture, leaving you in a constant fight-or-flight state. This can wreak havoc on your body, leading to issues like weight gain, anxiety, and even high blood pressure. It's like living in a perpetual state of panic, and your hormones are the ones paying the price.

Managing stress is crucial for keeping hormonal chaos at bay. Simple practices like deep breathing, meditation, or even a 30-minute walk in the park can help bring cortisol levels back down to a healthy range. Activities that bring you joy—whether it's painting, dancing, or gardening—also support this reset, helping your body regain balance. By managing stress, you're not only benefiting your adrenal glands but also allowing your entire hormonal system to work at its best.

Now, let's debunk the lie that all hormonal changes are negative. It's easy to think of hormones as the culprits behind every awkward teenage moment or pregnancy craving, but they play essential roles in our growth and adaptation. During puberty, hormonal changes are what turn us from gangly adolescents into (hopefully) well-adjusted adults. They drive the development of secondary sexual characteristics and are crucial for reproductive maturity. Think of these hormones as the architects of your adult body, laying the groundwork for everything from muscle mass to bone density. Pregnancy is another time when hormones take center stage, supporting the development of new life and preparing the body for childbirth. Far from being detrimental, these hormonal changes are vital for survival and adaptation.

Hormones also respond to environmental changes, helping us adapt to new situations. For instance, if you move to a high-altitude region, your body will increase the production of certain hormones to help you cope with the lower oxygen levels. These adaptive hormonal shifts are often overlooked but essential for our resilience and ability to thrive in diverse environments.

The truth is that hormones have a profound influence on our mental health, acting as the unseen conductors of our emotional orchestra. Remember serotonin, the "feel-good" hormone? It's key to maintaining mood stability, helping you handle life's highs and lows without feeling like you're on an emotional rollercoaster. When serotonin levels drop, it's often connected to depression, anxiety, and various other mood disorders.

And remember dopamine, the reward hormone that lights up your brain when you experience something pleasurable, like eating chocolate or achieving a goal. It's what makes you feel motivated and happy, encouraging you to repeat actions that bring joy. Postpartum depression is another example of how hormones can impact mental health. After childbirth, there's a significant drop in estrogen and progesterone, which can affect mood and lead to feelings of sadness or despair. Understanding the connection between hormones and mental health can empower you to seek support and interventions that promote emotional well-being.

Lastly, let's squash the misconception that hormonal health is only about reproduction. Yes, hormones are key players in the reproductive process, but their influence extends far beyond that. Take thyroid hormones, for instance. These are crucial for regulating metabolism and ensuring you have enough energy to go about your daily activities. They influence everything from heart rate to body temperature, acting like the body's internal thermostat. When thyroid hormones are out of balance, you might experience fatigue, weight changes, or even mood swings. Insulin is another hormone with a broader scope. It's responsible for regulating blood sugar levels, ensuring your body has a steady supply of energy. Without insulin, your cells would struggle to access glucose, leading to conditions like diabetes. Insulin plays a vital role in energy regulation, and maintaining balance is essential for overall health.

Understanding these truths and lies about hormones can help you navigate your health with confidence. It's about recognizing hormones' positive roles in adaptation and development, their critical influence on mental health, and the wide range of bodily functions they regulate. By dispelling these myths, you can take a more informed approach to your hormonal health, embracing the changes that come with it and seeking balance in every aspect of your life. With this newfound knowledge, you're better equipped to manage your health and embrace the complexities of your body's hormonal landscape.

As we wrap up this myth-busting chapter, remember that hormones are not the villains they're often made out to be. They're essential players in the grand theater of your life, contributing to everything from your mood to your metabolism. Understanding their roles and dispelling myths allows you to see the bigger picture of health. In the next chapter, we'll explore how self-care and routine establishment can further support your hormonal health, offering practical tips and strategies for a balanced and fulfilling life.

CHAPTER 14
SELF-CARE AND ROUTINE ESTABLISHMENT

You know that feeling when you're trying to juggle a million things at once, and suddenly, you drop the ball on the one thing you thought you had under control? Yep, that's your hormones when you don't have a routine. Imagine your body as a well-oiled machine, smoothly running on a schedule. But when the cogs are out of sync, it's like trying to drive a car with square wheels—you're not going far, and it's going to be a bumpy ride. Establishing a self-care routine can be the grease that keeps your hormonal machine running smoothly, reducing those unexpected bumps in the road.

Consistency is key in maintaining hormonal health, and routines play a pivotal role in achieving this stability. Just as you wouldn't randomly water a plant whenever you remember, your body thrives on predictable schedules. Synchronizing your daily activities with your natural circadian rhythms can help stabilize hormonal fluctuations and promote overall well-being. Your circadian rhythm, also known as your internal body clock, is responsible for regulating sleep-wake cycles, hormone release, and even digestion. According to a study published in PMC, aligning your lifestyle with these rhythms can support hormonal balance, improve sleep quality, and enhance energy levels throughout the day. Regular meal times are also crucial for supporting metabolic hormones like insulin, which thrive on consistency. Eating at similar times each day helps your body maintain stable blood sugar and energy levels, reducing those mid-afternoon crashes that make you reach for an extra shot of espresso or a sugary snack.

Creating a self-care routine tailored to your hormonal needs involves incorporating several key elements. First and foremost, make time for physical activity. I know I've mentioned this before, but it's worth repeating: Exercise not only helps with your waist-line but also significantly contributes to regulating hormones like cortisol and endorphins. Whether it's a brisk walk in the park, a yoga session, or a full-on gym workout, find what gets your heart pumping and stick with it. Equally important is scheduling regular relaxation and downtime. In today's fast-paced world, it's easy to forget the importance of unwinding. Incorporate activities that calm your mind and body, like reading, meditating, or soaking in a bubble bath with a glass of your favorite beverage. Balanced nutrition planning is another cornerstone of your routine. Ensure your diet includes a variety of nutrient-rich foods like fruits, vegetables, lean proteins, and whole grains, which support hormonal health and overall vitality.

Personalizing your self-care routine is not just a suggestion, it's a key to empowerment. We're all unique, with different hormonal needs, lifestyle factors, and stressors. Start by identifying your individual stressors and understanding how they impact your hormones. Is it work deadlines, family drama, or maybe the neighbor's barking dog at 3 a.m.? Identifying these stressors enables you to customize your routine to tackle them effectively, putting you in the driver's seat of your health. Adapt your schedule according to your hormonal cycles, whether it's the menstrual cycle or seasonal changes. For instance, you might find you need more rest and self-care during certain phases of your cycle. Paying attention to your body and adapting your routine can greatly impact your feelings, giving you a sense of control and confidence. Consider utilizing various tools and resources to help you establish and maintain an effective self-care routine. These tools are like a supportive friend, always there to lend a hand. Planners or scheduling apps can be invaluable for mapping out your day and ensuring you carve out time for self-care. Tools like Aloe Bud or Shleep, as highlighted in an article on CNET, can send gentle reminders to drink water, take breaks, or wind down for the night, keeping you on track even when life gets hectic. Journaling is another powerful tool for tracking your progress and identifying mood or energy patterns. By noting how you feel each day, you can gain insights into what works for you and make adjustments as needed. Lastly, don't overlook the value of community support groups for accountability. Whether it's an online forum, a local club, or a circle of friends, having a support network can inspire you to remain dedicated to your self-care goals.

Reflection Section: Routine Reset

- Routine Checklist: Sit down and design your ideal daily routine. Consider when you'll wake up, eat, exercise, and relax. Include activities that make you happy and promote balance. Write it down and commit to following it for a week, then reassess and tweak it as needed.

While investing time in creating a self-care routine may initially feel overwhelming, keep in mind that even small changes can lead to substantial enhancements in your hormonal health and overall well-being. By prioritizing consistency, embracing personalization, and leveraging helpful tools, you're not just on your way to creating a balanced lifestyle that supports your body's unique needs. You're also on the path to feeling proud and accomplished. Each day you stick to your routine, you're making a positive impact on your health and that's something to be proud of.

MINDFUL LIVING: A PATH TO HORMONAL HEALTH

Imagine you're sitting in traffic, mentally listing everything you need to do today. Meanwhile, your body is busy whipping up a cocktail of stress hormones. This is where mindfulness steps in. It's not just about surviving the chaos but thriving amidst it. Mindfulness is about being present and fully engaging with the moment. When it comes to hormonal health, mindfulness is like a soothing balm, reducing stress and supporting balance in your body's complex hormonal dance.

Mindfulness helps enhance emotional resilience, acting as a buffer against daily life stressors.By practicing mindfulness, you're training your brain to respond thoughtfully to stress instead of reacting impulsively. This reduces your body's stress responses, specifically lowering levels of cortisol, the infamous stress hormone. Think of cortisol as that annoying neighbor who blasts loud music at 2 a.m.—you don't want it to stick around for long. By reducing cortisol, mindfulness helps maintain hormonal balance, leaving you feeling calmer and more in control. Incorporating mindfulness into your daily life isn't about adding more to your plate; it's about savoring what's already there.

Integrating mindfulness into everyday routines can be both simple and transformative. Start with mindful eating, which is all about paying attention to your food and the experience of eating. Slow down, savor each bite, and notice the flavors and textures. This practice not only enhances digestion and satiety but also makes meals more enjoyable. It's like turning dinner into a mini-vacation for your senses.Breathing exercises are another effective method for quick stress relief. Try taking slow, deep breaths while concentrating on the feeling of air flowing in and out of your body. This simple act can calm your nervous system and reduce stress hormones faster than you can say "zen." Walking meditation is another way to practice mindfulness through movement. As you walk, focus on each step, the sensation of your feet touching the ground, and the rhythm of your breath. This practice not only keeps you grounded but also adds a touch of serenity to your day.

Creating an environment that supports mindfulness can significantly enhance its benefits for hormonal health. Start by decluttering your spaces. A cluttered environment can contribute to a cluttered mind, making it harder to relax and focus. Imagine your home as a peaceful retreat rather than a chaotic storage unit. Include natural elements such as plants and sunlight, as they can promote a calming atmosphere and enhance your mood. Plants brighten a room and purify the air, while natural light helps regulate your body's circadian rhythms. This combination creates a refreshing ambiance, fostering a sense of tranquility and well-being.

Mindfulness techniques specifically beneficial for hormonal regulation include body scan meditation, gratitude journaling, and visualization techniques.Body scan meditation entails directing your attention to various parts of your body and observing sensations without judgment. This practice fosters a connection with your physical self, encouraging relaxation and balance. Gratitude journaling shifts your focus from stress to appreciation, reducing stress levels and promoting positive emotions. Spend a few minutes each day writing down what you're grateful for, whether it's a sunny day or a delicious cup of coffee. Visualization techniques involve imagining peaceful scenes or scenarios, promoting relaxation and a sense of calm. Picture your stress melting away like ice cream on a hot day, leaving you refreshed and grounded.

Incorporating mindfulness into your life is like giving your body and mind a much-needed spa day without ever leaving home. It's not about achieving perfection but about finding moments of peace and presence amidst the busyness. As you embrace mindfulness, you may find your hormonal health improving alongside your well-being. This chapter invites you to explore, experiment, and enjoy the journey to a more mindful, balanced life.

CHAPTER 15
ADDRESSING COMMON HORMONAL CONDITIONS

Ah, hormones. Those tricky little devils can turn even the calmest among us into a whirlwind of emotion and confusion. One moment, you're on top of the world, and the next, you're crying because your favorite mug got chipped. Let's face it: hormones love to keep things interesting. But what happens when this hormonal dance turns into a chaotic rave? That's where conditions like Polycystic Ovary Syndrome, or PCOS, come into play. PCOS is not just a simple hormonal imbalance, it's a complex disorder that affects millions of women of childbearing age. It's like an unruly party crasher who shows up uninvited, messes with your playlist and leaves you with a mess to clean up. This complexity emphasizes the need for professional guidance and support in managing the condition.

PCOS is often like a hormonal symphony gone awry. It starts with elevated levels of androgens—those hormones typically found in higher amounts in men but necessary in small quantities for women, too. When these levels rise, they can lead to symptoms like hirsutism, which is a fancy term for unwanted hair growth in places you'd rather not have it, and acne that seems determined to revisit from your teenage years. The irregular menstrual cycles that accompany PCOS are like a calendar that refuses to stay on schedule, making it difficult to predict when Miss Flo might make an appearance. And let's not forget about the polycystic ovaries themselves, which can be spotted on an ultrasound, resembling a string of pearls—sounds pretty, but it's more of a nuisance than a necklace.

The impact of PCOS goes beyond just the physical symptoms. It's a condition that can affect your overall health and fertility, creating a ripple effect that touches various aspects of life.Women with PCOS are at a greater risk of developing type 2 diabetes because insulin resistance often occurs alongside the condition. This insulin resistance can make it challenging to shed unwanted pounds, leading to weight gain that feels as stubborn as a toddler refusing to eat their veggies. Fertility can also take a hit, as irregular ovulation makes conception feel like a game of chance rather than a well-planned milestone. The emotional impact is significant as well, with anxiety and depression often creeping in uninvited, adding further complexity to an already difficult condition.

Here's the good news: while there might not be a one-size-fits-all cure for PCOS, there are plenty of ways to manage and mitigate its symptoms. Lifestyle changes are often the first line of defense, with low-carbohydrate diets playing a starring role in regulating insulin levels. Imagine it as gently shifting the gears of your metabolism, helping it run more smoothly. Regular exercise is another key player, helping to lower insulin levels and improve symptoms while boosting your mood. When lifestyle changes alone are insufficient, medications can provide valuable assistance. Oral contraceptives can help regulate menstrual cycles and lower androgen levels, while anti-androgen medications specifically address those troublesome excess hormones, offering you greater control over your condition.

Testing for polycystic ovary syndrome (PCOS) typically begins with a visit to a healthcare provider who specializes in women's health. The process usually involves a comprehensive evaluation, including a detailed medical history, physical examination, and specific laboratory tests.During the consultation, the doctor will ask about menstrual irregularities, symptoms like excessive hair growth or acne, and any family history of hormonal disorders.

Following this initial assessment, blood tests may be conducted to check hormone levels, including androgens and insulin, and to rule out other conditions that could mimic PCOS. Additionally, an ultrasound may be performed to examine the ovaries for cysts and assess overall reproductive health. Based on the results from these tests, the healthcare provider can confirm a diagnosis and discuss potential treatment options tailored to the individual's needs. Regular follow-up appointments are also essential for managing symptoms and monitoring any changes in health, providing you with the reassurance that you are being cared for and your condition is being closely monitored.

PCOS might be an unwelcome guest, but with the right strategies and a bit of self-compassion, you can regain control and find balance. Whether it's through dietary adjustments, exercise, or medical interventions, managing PCOS is all about finding what works best for you. With effective management, you can lead a balanced life, free from the disruptive symptoms of PCOS. Remember, you're not alone in this journey—support is available, and knowledge is your greatest ally.

ENDOMETRIOSIS EXPLAINED: NAVIGATING SYMPTOMS AND TREATMENT OPTIONS

Endometriosis is a chronic condition in which tissue that resembles the lining of the uterus grows outside of it, often leading to pain and other complications. This misplaced tissue can cause inflammation, scar tissue, and adhesions, resulting in a variety of symptoms that can significantly affect a woman's quality of life. Common symptoms include painful periods (dysmenorrhea), pelvic pain, pain during intercourse, and abnormal bleeding. Some women may also experience gastrointestinal symptoms, such as bloating, diarrhea, or constipation, especially during their menstrual cycle. However, the severity of symptoms does not always correlate with the extent of the condition, as Some women with mild endometriosis may still suffer from intense pain. In contrast, others with advanced stages may have mild symptoms.

Diagnosing endometriosis typically requires a combination of approaches. A healthcare provider will typically start with a thorough medical history and physical examination, during which they may perform a pelvic exam to check for cysts or scars. Imaging tests, such as ultrasound or MRI, can help visualize cysts associated with endometriosis, although a definitive diagnosis usually requires a laparoscopy—a minimally invasive surgical procedure. During a laparoscopy, a surgeon can look for and possibly remove endometrial-like tissue, allowing for both diagnosis and treatment.

Treatment for endometriosis differs depending on the severity of symptoms and the woman's reproductive goals. For many, pain management can be achieved through over-the-counter nonsteroidal anti-inflammatory drugs (NSAIDs) or hormonal treatments, such as hormonal birth control methods, which can help regulate or eliminate menstruation and reduce pain. For those seeking to conceive, fertility treatments may be necessary, and certain surgical options can help remove endometrial tissue and adhesions to improve fertility chances.

In more severe cases where conservative treatments are ineffective, surgery may be recommended to remove endometriosis lesions and adhesions. This can involve excision, which removes the endometriosis tissue completely, or ablation, which destroys the tissue but may not eliminate it entirely. Although surgery can significantly reduce symptoms, it is essential for women to discuss the potential risks and benefits with their healthcare provider.

Ultimately, managing endometriosis is an ongoing process that may require a combination of medical treatment, lifestyle changes, and supportive care. Many women benefit from joining support groups where they can share experiences and coping strategies. Awareness and education about endometriosis are vital, as early diagnosis and effective treatment can significantly improve outcomes and help women lead healthier, more fulfilling lives.

OVARIAN CYSTS: UNDERSTANDING CAUSES, SYMPTOMS, AND TREATMENT

Ovarian cysts are fluid-filled sacs that can form on or within the ovaries, and they are relatively common among women of reproductive age. Most ovarian cysts are benign and typically arise during the menstrual cycle as part of the ovulation process. Functional cysts, such as follicular and luteal cysts, occur when the ovarian follicles do not release an egg or when the follicle closes after releasing the egg, leading to fluid accumulation. While many women may have cysts at some point in their lives, most do not experience any symptoms, and many cysts resolve on their own without treatment.

However, some ovarian cysts can cause noticeable symptoms, particularly if they become large or rupture. Common symptoms may include pelvic pain, pressure or heaviness in the abdomen, bloating, or changes in menstrual patterns. In some cases, women may experience pain during intercourse or exhibit symptoms of urinary urgency or frequency. If a cyst ruptures, it can lead to severe pain and internal bleeding, which requires immediate medical attention. Regular pelvic examinations and imaging tests, such as ultrasounds, can help detect the presence of cysts and monitor their development over time.

Treatment for ovarian cysts largely depends on the type of cyst, its size, and the symptoms it causes. For many functional cysts, the recommended approach may be watchful waiting, as they often resolve on their own within a few menstrual cycles. However, for persistent or symptomatic cysts, hormonal contraceptives may be prescribed to help prevent the formation of new cysts. Surgical intervention may be necessary in cases where cysts are large, causing severe symptoms, or are suspected to be malignant. This can involve laparoscopic surgery to remove the cyst or, in more severe cases, a more extensive surgery to remove the affected ovary.

Overall, while ovarian cysts are often harmless and manageable, it is essential for women to be aware of their symptoms and maintain regular check-ups with their healthcare providers. Understanding ovarian cysts and their implications can help women make informed decisions about their reproductive health and seek appropriate care when necessary.

OVARIAN CANCER AWARENESS: SYMPTOMS, DIAGNOSIS, AND SUPPORT

Ovarian cancer is a serious and often silent disease that affects women.It happens when abnormal cells in the ovaries grow uncontrollably, which can result in tumor formation. One of the challenges with ovarian cancer is that its symptoms can be vague and easily attributed to other conditions, making early detection difficult. Common symptoms can include ongoing abdominal bloating, trouble eating or feeling full rapidly, pelvic or abdominal pain, and alterations in urinary habits, such as heightened urgency or frequency. Women experiencing these symptoms, particularly if they persist for more than a few weeks, should consult a healthcare provider for further evaluation.

The diagnosis of ovarian cancer usually includes a combination of pelvic examinations, imaging tests like ultrasounds or CT scans, and blood tests to measure levels of the tumor marker CA-125. A definitive diagnosis often requires a biopsy, which can be performed during a surgical procedure. Early-stage ovarian cancer may be asymptomatic, which is why regular gynecological check-ups and being aware of family history are crucial for women, especially those with risk factors such as age, genetic predisposition (e.g., BRCA1 or BRCA2 mutations), or a personal history of breast or colorectal cancer.

Support is essential for women diagnosed with ovarian cancer, as the journey can be emotionally and physically challenging. Treatment options vary based on the stage of the cancer and may include surgery, chemotherapy, and targeted therapy. Support groups and counseling services can provide emotional assistance, while resources like the Ovarian Cancer Research Alliance and the National Ovarian Cancer Coalition offer valuable information and community support. Additionally, women can benefit from connecting with other survivors, which can foster a sense of hope and resilience during their treatment journey.

Raising awareness about ovarian cancer is vital for promoting early detection and improving outcomes. Education about the signs and symptoms and regular check-ups can empower women to advocate for their health. With advances in research and treatment options, there is hope for those affected by this disease, underscoring the importance of support networks and community engagement in the fight against ovarian cancer.

UNDERSTANDING DIABETES: SYMPTOMS, COMPLICATIONS, AND SELF-MANAGEMENT

Diabetes is a chronic condition marked by elevated blood glucose levels due to the body's inability to produce or properly utilize insulin, a hormone crucial for converting glucose into energy. It is also the most common hormonal disorder in the United States. There are mainly two types of diabetes: Type 1, which is usually diagnosed in children and young adults, where the body produces little or no insulin, and Type 2, which usually develops in adults and is frequently linked to obesity and a lack of physical activity, leading to insulin resistance. Recognizing the symptoms of diabetes is crucial for early diagnosis and managementCommon symptoms include excessive thirst and urination, as well as extreme fatigue, blurred vision, and slow-healing wounds. If not addressed, diabetes can result in serious complications that can impact multiple organs and systems throughout the body.

Complications of diabetes can be significant and varied. Long-term high blood sugar levels can harm the cardiovascular system, elevating the risk of heart disease and stroke.Diabetic neuropathy, which refers to nerve damage, can lead to pain, tingling, or a loss of sensation, especially in the feet and hands. Other complications may include kidney disease, eye problems such as diabetic retinopathy, and increased susceptibility to infections. The cumulative effect of these complications can lead to a decreased quality of life and, in severe cases, may necessitate amputations or dialysis.

Self-management is vital to diabetes care and involves lifestyle changes, monitoring, and medication management. Individuals with diabetes should aim to maintain stable blood sugar levels through a balanced diet rich in whole grains, fruits, vegetables, and lean proteins while limiting processed sugars and carbohydrates. Regular physical activity is also essential; it helps improve insulin sensitivity and overall health. Monitoring blood sugar levels regularly allows individuals to understand how different foods, activities, and stress levels affect their diabetes, empowering them to make informed decisions about their care.

Education and support are key in managing diabetes effectively. Diabetes self-management education programs provide individuals with the knowledge and skills needed to navigate their condition confidently. Additionally, connecting with healthcare professionals, dietitians, and support groups can offer encouragement and strategies for coping with the challenges of living with diabetes. As diabetes awareness continues to grow, so does the understanding of how to live well with this condition, emphasizing that proactive management can significantly reduce the risk of complications and enhance overall well-being.

HYPOTHYROIDISM AND HYPERTHYROIDISM: A GUIDE

Imagine your thyroid as your body's thermostat, keeping your energy and metabolism at just the right level. But what happens when that thermostat goes rogue? We find ourselves in the realm of thyroid disorders, specifically hypothyroidism and hyperthyroidism. Hypothyroidism, often caused by Hashimoto's disease, is like setting your thermostat too low, leaving you feeling sluggish and cold. Hashimoto's is an autoimmune condition where your body mistakenly attacks the thyroid, akin to having a security system that identifies your own keys as a threat. On the flip side, hyperthyroidism, frequently linked to Graves' disease, is like cranking the thermostat to the max. With Graves', your immune system goes into overdrive, turning your thyroid into a caffeine-fueled dynamo. Both conditions significantly impact your metabolism and energy levels, leaving you either trudging through molasses or bouncing off the walls.

Symptoms of these conditions are as distinct as night and day. Hypothyroidism might have you feeling like a sleepy bear in hibernation. Common symptoms include fatigue, weight gain, and a sensitivity to cold that leaves you layered in sweaters even in summer. Your skin might become dry, and your mood could take a nosedive, contributing to a general sense of blah. On the other hand, hyperthyroidism kicks things into high gear, often resulting in anxiety, unexplained weight loss, and a heat intolerance that makes even a cool breeze feel like a furnace blast. You might find yourself with a racing heart or difficulty sleeping, turning you into the Energizer Bunny with a side of insomnia. Diagnosing these conditions involves blood tests measuring thyroid-stimulating hormone (TSH), Free T4, and Free and reverse T3 levels. Think of these tests as a report card for your thyroid, providing crucial information on its performance.

Managing hypothyroidism typically involves hormone replacement therapy. Your body absorbs a synthetic version of T4 (levothyroxine), which is then converted into the active thyroid hormone T3. Then, you have a desiccated thyroid replacement therapy (Armour Thyroid or NP Thyroid are the big-name brands) that is 80% T4 and 20% T3. Hormone replacement option steps in to help regulate your body's energy use, like a personal energy manager ensuring everything runs smoothly. Regular thyroid function tests are crucial to monitoring your hormone levels, ensuring the dosage remains right. It's like keeping an eye on the thermostat to maintain a comfortable environment. Dietary considerations also play a role in managing the condition. Iodine is essential for thyroid hormone production in foods like fish and dairy. However, it's a delicate balance—too much iodine can exacerbate problems, so moderation is key.

Hyperthyroidism requires a slightly different approach. Anti-thyroid drugs, such as methimazole, can help reduce thyroid hormone production, akin to turning the dial down on our overactive thermostat. These medications help manage symptoms and bring the thyroid back to a more manageable pace. For some, radioactive iodine therapy might be recommended.This treatment consists of ingesting a small dose of radioactive iodine, which targets and gradually shrinks the overactive thyroid tissue, dialing back the hormone production. While it might sound a bit like science fiction, it's a proven method for reining in a hyperactive thyroid. Lifestyle changes, particularly stress management techniques, are vital in reducing symptoms. Practices like yoga or meditation can help calm the nervous system, offering relief from the whirlwind of symptoms.

ADRENAL FATIGUE: MYTH OR REALITY?

Picture this: it's the middle of the afternoon, and you're feeling more exhausted than a cat after a full day of chasing laser pointers. You've had your coffee, you slept okay last night, but you're still dragging. You've heard whispers about "adrenal fatigue," which sounds like the perfect explanation for your chronic tiredness. But here's the kicker—adrenal fatigue is a bit of a controversial topic in the medical world. It's like the Bigfoot of health conditions; plenty of people talk about it, but the evidence is elusive.

The idea of adrenal fatigue centers around the notion that chronic stress wears out your adrenal glands, the little guys above your kidneys responsible for producing stress hormones like cortisol. When life throws too much stress your way, these glands supposedly get overworked and can't keep up, leading to a slew of symptoms like chronic exhaustion, sleep disturbances, and brain fog. Imagine it as running a marathon without training; eventually, your body just decides it's had enough.

Despite its popularity in wellness circles, the medical community remains divided on the legitimacy of adrenal fatigue as a diagnosis. Critics argue that the symptoms often attributed to adrenal fatigue could be explained by other conditions or lifestyle factors. Unlike Addison's disease, which involves actual damage to the adrenal glands, adrenal fatigue lacks definitive clinical evidence. It's like trying to solve a mystery without all the clues. Researchers have found inconsistencies in cortisol levels among those who claim to have adrenal fatigue, leading to skepticism about its validity as a standalone condition.

So, what's really going on if adrenal fatigue isn't officially recognized? Chronic stress plays a massive role in how our bodies function, leading to hormonal imbalances, including dysregulated cortisol production. When cortisol levels stay too high or too low for too long, it can throw off your whole system, leaving you feeling like you need a nap. Lifestyle factors, such as poor diet, lack of exercise, and inadequate sleep, can exacerbate these stress-induced symptoms, making you feel like you're in a cycle of fatigue.

Now, let's talk solutions. While the jury is still out on adrenal fatigue, there are practical steps you can take to support adrenal health and manage stress effectively. First things first, focus on balanced nutrition and hydration. A diet rich in whole foods, lean proteins, and healthy fats can provide the nutrients your body needs to function optimally. Think of it as giving your body the premium fuel it deserves. Staying hydrated is equally important, as dehydration can worsen fatigue and stress levels. Regular physical activity is another key player in adrenal health. But there's no need to train for a marathon; choose exercises that match your energy levels, whether it's a leisurely walk, a gentle yoga session, or a Zumba class that gets your heart pumping.

Mind-body practices like yoga and meditation can also reduce stress and promote adrenal health. These practices help calm the mind, regulate breathing, and lower cortisol levels, allowing your body to relax and recharge. Incorporating these stress-reduction techniques into your daily routine can create a buffer against the effects of chronic stress, giving your adrenals a much-needed break. Remember, while adrenal fatigue might be debated, the impact of stress on your health is very real. You can reclaim your energy and vitality by taking steps to manage stress and support your body's well-being.

As we conclude our examination of hormonal conditions, it becomes evident that recognizing and addressing these imbalances can greatly influence your overall health. From PCOS to thyroid disorders and even the enigmatic adrenal fatigue, each condition offers unique challenges and opportunities for better living. There are many other hormone disorders and diseases that haven't been discussed in this book, but my focus was on the most prevalent ones affecting both women and men. Now that we've tackled these hormonal hurdles let's move on to something a bit more uplifting—how to empower yourself with the knowledge and tools needed to maintain hormonal harmony.

CHAPTER 16
EMPOWERING YOURSELF THROUGH KNOWLEDGE

Ever feel like you're navigating the vast ocean of hormonal health with nothing more than a leaky rowboat and a questionable map? You're not alone. Many of us have felt like castaways on this journey, desperately trying to decipher our bodies' mysterious signals. The good news? You don't need to be a medical expert to take charge of your hormonal health. All it takes is a little self-advocacy and the right information. Imagine yourself as the captain of your own ship, bravely steering through the waves of hormonal confusion toward the shores of understanding and empowerment. By taking control of your hormonal health, you're not just navigating, you're leading the way. It's time to dive into what self-advocacy means in the context of hormonal health and how you can become your own best advocate.

SELF-ADVOCACY IN HORMONAL HEALTH

Understanding self-advocacy in hormonal health is like discovering a hidden superpower. It's about taking the reins, educating yourself about your body, and ensuring that your voice is heard loud and clear in every medical appointment. Begin by arming yourself with knowledge. Dive into resources that explain your specific hormonal concerns, whether it's thyroid issues, menopause, or insulin resistance. Knowledge truly is power, and being informed about your health conditions enables you to make decisions confidently. Speaking up during medical appointments is crucial. Imagine yourself as the protagonist in your health story, not a side character. Be ready to ask questions, share your symptoms, and express any concerns. You deserve to have your perspective considered and your health prioritized. Don't be afraid to fire your doctor and find another one if you don't feel they take your concerns seriously, or just try to shove prescriptions on top of prescriptions you.

Building confidence in health discussions doesn't happen overnight but is a skill worth developing. Start by preparing questions and topics in advance. Jot down anything you want to discuss with your healthcare provider, from specific symptoms to treatment options. This preparation ensures that you don't leave the appointment with a head full of unasked questions and potential "aha" moments. Practicing assertive communication techniques can also help you feel more confident. Assertive communication is about expressing your needs clearly and respectfully. For example, instead of saying 'I think my treatment is not working ', you can say 'I feel that my symptoms are not improving, and I'd like to explore alternative treatments.' Being assertive isn't about being confrontational; it's about ensuring your voice is heard and your needs are met.

Accessing reliable information is your compass in the sea of hormonal health. In an age where misinformation is as common as cat videos, evaluating online health resources for credibility is crucial. Stick to reputable websites, such as those ending in .gov, .edu, or recognized health organizations. Look for articles backed by scientific studies and written by qualified professionals. Recognizing red flags in health misinformation is equally important. Be wary of sensational headlines, miracle cures, or sources that lack citations. If something sounds too good to be true, it probably is. Trustworthy information is the foundation of effective self-advocacy, providing you with a sense of security and helping you make informed decisions that align with your health goals.

Overcoming barriers to advocacy may feel like tackling a labyrinth, but it's entirely possible with the right approach. One common obstacle is navigating complex medical jargon. Don't hesitate to ask your healthcare provider to explain the terms in plain language. Remember, you're not expected to be a walking medical dictionary. It's their job to ensure you understand your health. Another hurdle is managing time constraints during appointments. With the clock ticking, it's easy to feel rushed. However, by preparing questions and topics in advance, you can ensure that you're proactive and ready to make the most of your appointment. Prioritize your most pressing concerns and share them at the start of the appointment, ensuring that essential topics are addressed. If time runs short, request a follow-up appointment or additional resources to review at your leisure.

Reflection Section: Your Self-Advocacy Checklist

- Understand Your Health: Identify one area of hormonal health you'd like to explore further. Research reputable sources and jot down key takeaways.
- Prepare for Appointments: List three questions or concerns you have about your hormonal health. Bring this list to your next doctor's visit.

With these strategies in hand, you're better equipped to navigate the complexities of hormonal health.

SEEKING PROFESSIONAL HELP: WHAT TO ASK YOUR DOCTOR

Getting ready for a medical appointment can sometimes feel like prepping for a big exam. There's a lot to consider, and you want to ensure you cover all your bases. But here's the thing: preparation is your best ally in navigating the often complex world of hormonal health. Start by clearly listing any symptoms and concerns. Whether it's a sudden drop in energy, unexplained weight changes, or mood swings that rival a telenovela, jot everything down. This list will serve as your roadmap during the appointment, ensuring that nothing important slips through the cracks. Don't forget to bring a list of any medications and supplements you're taking. Even that herbal tea you sip every night counts. These details can provide your doctor with essential context, helping them piece together the bigger picture of your health.

Once you're in the appointment, it's time to play detective. Asking the right questions is key to understanding your health. Begin by inquiring about the potential causes of your symptoms. Is it just a case of too much stress, or could it be more complex, like a hormonal imbalance, which is a condition where the body produces too much or too little of a certain hormone? Understanding the root cause is crucial for effective treatment. Next, dive into discussions about treatment options and their side effects. While medication can be a wonder drug for some, others might lean towards natural therapies. It's important to weigh the pros and cons of each approach. Also, ask about necessary diagnostic tests. Whether it's blood work or imaging, understanding what's required will give you a clearer idea of the path ahead and help you prepare mentally and physically.

Understanding your diagnosis can sometimes feel like trying to read a foreign language without a dictionary. Don't be shy about requesting clarification on medical terms. Your health is too important to be left in a fog of medical jargon. Ask your doctor to explain things in plain language and, if possible, request written materials or resources to take home. This way, you'll have something to refer back to, ensuring you fully grasp the implications of your diagnosis. Remember, a diagnosis is not just a label. It's a guide to what's happening in your body and a stepping stone to finding the right solutions.

Exploring treatment options is where you get to play a more active role in your health journey. It's not just about choosing between medication and natural therapies; it's about finding what works best for you. Compare the potential benefits of medication against the appeal of natural therapies, such as herbal supplements, acupuncture, or dietary changes. Each has its merits, and sometimes a combination approach can offer the best results. Discuss the role of diet and exercise in your treatment plan. These lifestyle changes can sometimes wield as much power as a prescription, helping to restore balance and improve overall well-being. Your doctor can offer guidance tailored to your specific needs, but it's up to you to implement these changes in your daily life.

Reflection Section: Doctor's Visit Prep List

- Symptom Log: Keep a diary for a week prior to your appointment, noting any symptoms, their frequency, and severity.
- Key Questions: Write down at least three questions you want to ask your doctor, focusing on the most pressing issues.
- Treatment Preferences: Consider your treatment preferences and jot down any therapies you're interested in exploring.

By approaching your medical appointments with a clear plan and an open mind, you can confidently navigate the complexities of hormonal health.

TRACKING AND MONITORING YOUR HORMONAL HEALTH

Imagine having a detective's notebook, tracking clues about your body's mysterious behaviors. That's essentially what self-monitoring your hormonal health is all about. By keeping tabs on your hormonal health metrics, you gain insights that can help you connect the dots between how you feel and what's happening inside your body. This proactive approach allows you to identify patterns and triggers of symptoms. Maybe you've noticed that you crave sweets more than usual every time you're stressed, or perhaps your energy levels plummet right before your cycle.

Capturing these patterns helps you understand your body better and enhances communication with your healthcare provider. When you can present clear data, the conversation becomes more productive, like bringing a map to a treasure hunt.

In today's world, technology is your best friend when it comes to tracking hormonal health. Health apps designed for tracking menstrual cycles can provide invaluable insights. They can predict your cycle, helping you anticipate mood changes or cravings. Wearable devices are another fantastic tool. These gadgets monitor sleep and activity, providing a comprehensive view of your lifestyle and its impact on your hormones. Imagine waking up, checking your device, and understanding why you feel groggy or energized. Digital journals are equally crucial for those who prefer a more hands-on approach. Recording dietary habits and noting how different foods affect your mood or energy levels can offer a wealth of information. Each tool helps paint a fuller picture of how your body responds to various influences, making it easier to adjust your habits for better health.

Once you've gathered all this data, the next step is learning how to interpret it. Start by analyzing trends over time. Maybe you notice that your energy dips consistently at the same point in your cycle, or perhaps certain foods trigger bloating or fatigue. You can pinpoint what might be causing the fluctuations by correlating symptoms with lifestyle factors. Understanding these connections is like solving a puzzle—it gives you the power to make informed decisions about your health. For instance, if you realize that cutting back on caffeine improves your sleep quality, that's a change you can control. These insights can empower you to tweak your diet, exercise, or sleep habits to support your hormonal balance.

However, there may be times when your self-monitoring data raises red flags, indicating the need for professional evaluation. If you notice persistent or worsening symptoms or significant changes in your health metrics, it's time to consult your healthcare provider. Maybe your usual energy slump has evolved into constant fatigue, or unexplained weight changes have occurred despite no changes in diet or activity. These could be signs of an underlying issue that requires medical attention. Remember, while self-monitoring is a valuable tool, it's not a substitute for professional medical advice. Use your data as a conversation starter with your healthcare provider to explore potential solutions together.

Taking control of your hormonal health can feel empowering. By tracking and monitoring your hormones, you're taking an active role in your well-being and learning to understand your body's unique rhythm. The information you gather can guide lifestyle changes, help you communicate effectively with healthcare providers, and provide early warning signs when things might be going off track. Now that you've got a handle on monitoring your hormonal health, it's time to look at future directions in hormonal health, where exciting advancements are on the horizon.

CHAPTER 17
FUTURE DIRECTIONS IN HORMONAL HEALTH

Picture this: hormones, those mischievous little messengers, are like the Wi-Fi of your body—always working in the background, making sure everything runs smoothly. But just like with your home Wi-Fi, sometimes there's a glitch, and you're left wondering why things aren't working as they should. Enter the future of hormone replacement therapy (HRT), where the goal is to ensure that your body's network is running at top speed. HRT has come a long way from its early days, evolving from synthetic hormones that acted more like a bull in a china shop to bioidentical hormones that fit your body like a glove. These bioidentical hormones, crafted to mimic the exact structure of your natural hormones, aim to reduce side effects while enhancing efficacy. Researchers are also developing targeted HRT formulations that promise a more personalized approach, tailoring treatments to your unique needs and making the prospect of hormone therapy less daunting and more effective.

But the innovation doesn't stop there. Say goodbye to the days of popping pills with their uncertain absorption rates. Welcome to the future, where delivery methods are getting a high-tech makeover. Imagine microneedle patches that deliver hormones transdermally, bypassing the digestive system and offering a steady release directly through the skin. It's like having a tiny, invisible hormone fairy working round-the-clock. For those who prefer a more hands-off approach, hormone-releasing implants and injectables offer longer-lasting solutions, reducing the need for frequent doses and making life a tad bit simpler.

Of course, with great power comes great responsibility, and the scientific community is hard at work to ensure that HRT is as safe as it is effective. Personalized HRT regimens are being developed, taking into account individual risk factors to minimize side effects. Longitudinal studies are in the works, digging deep into the long-term effects of HRT to ensure that what you're putting into your body today won't come back to bite you tomorrow. It's like having a crystal ball that predicts the future and makes sure it's good, providing you with the confidence and security in the safety of your treatment.

Reflection Section: Future You, Today

- Visualize: Imagine a version of you, ten years from now, benefiting from these advancements in HRT. What does your life look like? How have these changes improved your health and well-being? Reflect on how embracing the future of HRT could enhance your daily life.

Looking ahead, the potential applications of HRT stretch beyond traditional uses. Imagine utilizing HRT to manage cognitive decline in aging populations, offering hope for maintaining mental sharpness as the years roll by. The future of HRT is bright, promising a world where your body's internal Wi-Fi is always at full bars, keeping everything connected and functioning just as it should. This potential for managing cognitive decline can bring a sense of hope and optimism about the future of your health.

ADVANCES IN PERSONALIZED HORMONAL TREATMENTS

That's the magic of precision medicine in hormonal health. It's all about considering the unique genetic, environmental, and lifestyle factors that make you, well, you. These factors could include your family history of certain diseases, your diet and exercise habits, and even your stress levels. This approach tailors treatments based on your specific hormone profiles, making it possible to address your needs more accurately. Think of it as having a personal hormonal GPS guiding you toward optimal health rather than just a generic map that could lead to a dead end or a cliff.

Thanks to genomic and epigenomic research, we're learning more about the intricate dance of our genes and how they affect hormone metabolism. Scientists are identifying genetic variants that can influence how your body processes hormones. These insights are like finding out that your body prefers classical music over rock and roll, enabling healthcare providers to tweak treatments accordingly. Epigenetic markers, which are changes in gene expression that don't involve altering the DNA sequence, are also shedding light on how lifestyle and environmental factors can impact hormone-related diseases. It's like discovering that your genes have a dimmer switch, which can be turned up or down based on lifestyle choices. This knowledge allows for a more nuanced approach to treatment, offering the potential to prevent or mitigate the impacts of certain hormonal disorders.

Biomarkers are becoming the Sherlock Holmes of personalized hormonal treatments, providing clues that help predict how you'll respond to therapy. These biological indicators can reveal the effectiveness of a treatment, enabling adjustments to be made for better results. Imagine having a dashboard that shows real-time updates on your hormone levels, helping guide decisions on what to tweak or what's working perfectly. By analyzing these biomarkers, doctors can craft individualized strategies that offer the best outcomes with the least side effects. This reassures you about the precision and effectiveness of your treatment, making you feel confident and secure in your healthcare journey.

The implications for patient care are profound. Personalized hormonal treatments promise to reduce adverse effects and improve adherence to therapy, which is a win-win for everyone involved. When treatments are tailored to fit individual needs, patients experience higher satisfaction and are more likely to stick to their prescribed plans. This approach transforms healthcare from a guessing game into a well-directed symphony where each part plays harmoniously with the others. Just imagine leaving a doctor's appointment feeling understood and confident that your treatment is specifically designed for you, not just anyone who walks through the door.

INNOVATIVE TECHNOLOGIES FOR HORMONAL HEALTH MONITORING

Imagine strolling through your day, not a care in the world, with a little device on your wrist, quietly keeping tabs on your hormones. It sounds like something out of a sci-fi movie, right? Well, welcome to the age of wearable technology—a game-changer in the realm of hormonal health. Smartwatches have evolved beyond counting steps and buzzing with notifications. They can now track hormone levels, providing real-time insights into your body's inner workings. Picture a tiny lab strapped to your wrist, giving you updates on your hormonal well-being while you're sipping your morning coffee or taking a leisurely walk in the park. But it's not just about the watches. Enter wearable biosensors, those nifty little gadgets designed for continuous monitoring. These sensors work tirelessly, collecting data and transmitting it to your smartphone, helping you make informed decisions about your health. It's like having a personal health assistant minus the hourly rate.

Gone are the days of cringing at the thought of a needle prick for a blood test. Say hello to non-invasive monitoring techniques, making hormone assessments as easy as brushing your teeth. Saliva-based hormone testing kits are gaining popularity, offering a painless alternative to traditional blood draws. Just a quick swab, and you've got a snapshot of your hormonal landscape. Imagine being able to check your hormone levels as easily as checking the weather forecast. And let's not forget about urine hormone monitoring strips, offering another painless method to keep track of those pesky hormones. These innovations provide convenience without compromising accuracy, making it easier than ever to stay in tune with your body's needs.

The integration of these technologies with digital health platforms is where the real magic happens. Apps that sync with your wearables offer personalized health insights, turning raw data into actionable information. It's like having a health coach in your pocket, always ready with advice and tips. Telemedicine platforms are also stepping up, utilizing hormonal data for remote consultations. Imagine discussing your hormone levels with a healthcare provider from the comfort of your home; no waiting room is required. The fusion of technology and healthcare creates a holistic approach to managing hormonal health, where data-driven decisions lead the way.

Of course, with great technology comes great responsibility. Data privacy and security concerns are at the forefront, ensuring that your personal information remains personal. As with any tech, ensuring the accuracy and reliability of consumer-grade devices is crucial. No one wants a smartwatch that makes you panic over a false alarm. These challenges highlight the importance of choosing reputable devices and platforms, ensuring that the technology you rely on is both trustworthy and effective. As we continue to embrace these innovations, finding the balance between convenience and safety is key.

THE NEXT FRONTIER: HORMONES AND GENETIC RESEARCH

Imagine a world where your genes are the scriptwriters of your hormonal play, determining every scene and plot twist. Genetic research is like a backstage pass, unveiling the complex interplay between our genes and hormonal regulation. Scientists are uncovering hormone-related genetic mutations that predispose some folks to hormonal imbalances, much like finding out your favorite sitcom has a hidden spin-off. These genetic predispositions can explain why some people breeze through life with hormonal harmony while others feel like they're starring in a never-ending hormonal soap opera. Understanding these genetic nuances offers the potential for more targeted interventions, helping to rewrite the script for those struggling with hormonal disorders.

Enter gene editing technologies, like the rock star CRISPR. This tool can potentially treat hormonal disorders by correcting genetic mutations at their source, like fixing a typo in your life's script before it hits the big screen. CRISPR can edit genes responsible for endocrine diseases, potentially providing a permanent solution rather than a temporary fix. Researchers are also using CRISPR in models to study hormonal pathways, offering insights into how these pathways interact and where they go awry. It's like having a blueprint of your body's hormonal wiring, allowing scientists to experiment with different rewiring strategies for better health outcomes.

Pharmacogenomics is another innovation that's making waves in hormone therapy, focusing on tailoring treatments to individual genetic profiles. By identifying genetic markers that affect drug metabolism, healthcare providers can customize hormone dosages to suit your unique genetic makeup. It's like having a personalized hormonal cocktail mixed for you, ensuring maximum efficacy and minimal side effects. This approach promises to reduce the trial-and-error aspect of hormone therapy, making it more like a precision-guided missile than a shot in the dark. As researchers continue to map these genetic markers, the future of hormone therapy looks brighter and more individualized.

Despite these exciting prospects, the application of genetic research in hormonal health comes with its fair share of ethical and regulatory challenges. Consent and genetic privacy are top concerns, as the ability to edit genes raises questions about who should have the power to alter our genetic makeup. Balancing innovation with ethical oversight is crucial to ensure that advancements in genetic research benefit everyone without compromising individual rights. As we navigate this brave new world, finding the right balance between progress and ethics will be key to harnessing the full potential of genetic research in hormonal health.

As we wrap up this chapter, consider how the intersection of genetics and hormones could redefine your approach to health. From CRISPR's precision editing to pharmacogenomics' tailored therapies, the possibilities are as vast as they are exciting. Embrace the future with open arms and a curious mind, ready to explore the next chapter of hormonal health.

CONCLUSION

Well, here we are at the finish line of our hormone-filled journey! If you've made it this far, give yourself a big pat on the back. You've braved the wild world of hormones, and hopefully, you've come out the other side with a clearer understanding and a few laughs along the way. Let's take a quick stroll down memory lane and revisit what we've learned.

First, we dove into the fascinating world of hormones, those tiny powerhouses that orchestrate everything from mood swings to metabolism. We explored the various roles they play in your body and how keeping them in balance is crucial for your well-being. We've also covered the importance of integrating Eastern and Western practices, combining ancient wisdom with modern science to give you the best of both worlds.

Diet and lifestyle changes were big stars in this book, too. We talked about how what you eat and how you live can significantly impact your hormonal harmony. We've covered a lot, from the superfoods that can boost your hormones to the exercises that get them dancing. And let's not forget the power of mindfulness and self-care routines to keep stress hormones like cortisol in check.

One of the most empowering realizations from our journey is that understanding your hormones isn't just about avoiding mood swings or managing weight. It's about taking control and empowering yourself to live a healthier, more balanced life. Remember, small changes can lead to big results. Maybe start by swapping out that sugary snack for a handful of nuts or squeezing in a few minutes of meditation each morning. Track these changes, see how they make you feel, and adjust as necessary. It's about building a lifestyle that supports your unique hormonal needs.

Now, I'm not going to sugarcoat it—taking charge of your hormonal health is an ongoing journey that takes effort. But you're not alone in this. You now have the knowledge and strategies to steer your own ship. Keep learning, stay curious, and don't hesitate to try new things. Maybe there's a yoga class waiting for you or an herbal tea you haven't yet sipped. Stay open to the possibilities and remain engaged in your journey.

Looking ahead, the future of hormonal health is bright. Research is ongoing, and new discoveries are happening all the time. These advancements will continue to shed light on our understanding and management of hormones. Stay informed and engaged. Join communities or subscribe to updates on the latest developments. Knowledge is power, and staying informed is key to keeping your health on track.

On a personal note, thank you for joining me on this journey. Writing this book has been a labor of love, and I'm grateful to share it with you. As someone who's been passionate about demystifying hormones, it's been a joy to see these topics come to life in a way that's accessible and, hopefully, a little fun. I remember when I first started unraveling the mysteries of hormones—it felt like trying to solve a puzzle without all the pieces. But with time and learning, things started to fall into place, and I hope the same happens for you. Remember, this journey is not just about health, it's about finding joy and fun in the process.

So, here's to continued learning and self-care. May your hormonal journey be filled with balance, health, and maybe a few dance parties along the way. Cheers to you and the exciting path ahead!

A SPECIAL REQUEST FOR YOUR FEEDBACK

Thank you for diving into the fascinating world of hormones with me! I hope this book has offered you valuable insights into the roles and rhythms of your body's hormones, giving you the knowledge to make empowered choices for your health and well-being. Whether you're looking to balance energy levels, improve mood, or simply understand the signals your body sends every day, I trust that these pages have brought a fresh perspective to the complex but captivating science of hormones.

Your feedback is invaluable. If you enjoyed this book or found it helpful, please consider leaving a review. Sharing your thoughts not only supports my work but also helps other readers who are curious about understanding their own hormone health. Thank you for being a part of this journey—your health, happiness, and harmony are what inspired every page.

How to Leave a Review:

1. You can visit the website where you purchased the book to leave a review.
2. Or scan the QR code that will take you to the review page on Amazon.
3. Share your thoughts—whether it's a few sentences or a detailed review, every bit helps!

With gratitude,

- Eliza Sharpe

GLOSSARY

Alpha cells- are endocrine cells in the pancreas that produce and release glucagon, a hormone that increases blood glucose levels.

Ashwagandha-an adaptogenic herb to help reduce cortisol levels and stress.

Ayurveda-The ancient Indian medical system, is based on ancient writings that rely on a "natural" and holistic approach to physical and mental health. Ayurvedic medicine is one of the world's oldest medical systems and remains one of India's traditional healthcare systems.

Beta cells-Endocrine cells in the pancreas that produce insulin, a hormone that regulates blood sugar levels.

Biofeedback-is a mind-body technique that helps you gain control over certain bodily functions, like heart rate, breathing, and muscle activity. During a biofeedback session, small sensors are placed around your wrist, ankles and head to provide real-time information about these functions.

Blood glucose levels- is the amount of glucose in a person's blood.

Cholecystokinin- a hormone that plays a key role in the digestion of fat and protein.

Dinacharya-The tradition of dinacharya (daily routine) is one of the single most powerful Ayurvedic tools for improving overall health and wellbeing.

Dopaminergic pathways- tracts in the brain that release dopamine, a neurotransmitter that plays a role in many functions, including movement, emotion, reward, and cognition.

Duodenum-is the first part of your small intestine. Its main job is to transform the partially digested food it receives from your stomach into nutrients your body can use.

Epigenomic-the study of the epigenome, which is the collection of chemical modifications to a cell's DNA and histone proteins. These modifications, known as epigenetic changes, can alter how genes are turned on and off without changing the DNA sequence.

Estrogen-a hormone that plays a key role in the development and maintenance of female sexual characteristics and reproductive health.

Follicle-stimulating hormone-is a hormone that regulates sexual development and reproduction in both men and women.

Genomic-the study of an organism's genome, or complete set of DNA, including all of its genes.

Glycogen-is a complex carbohydrate that stores glucose, the body's main energy source, in the liver and muscles. The body breaks down glycogen to release glucose into the bloodstream when it needs a quick energy boost or isn't getting glucose from food.

Glycemic index of foods- is a measure certain foods and how quickly it raises blood sugar levels after eating.

Glycogenolysis- is the process of breaking down glycogen into glucose to produce energy.

Gluconeogenesis- is a metabolic process that produces glucose from non-carbohydrate sources, such as lipids and proteins. It occurs in the liver and kidneys to maintain blood glucose levels, especially between meals.

Goitrogens- are substances found in certain foods. When consumed in excess, they can interfere with the function of the thyroid gland.

Gonadotropin- Are hormones that regulate the development, growth, and reproduction of the body. They are essential for normal sexual development, growth, and reproduction.

Human chorionic gonadotropin (hCG)- is a hormone mainly produced by the syncytiotrophoblastic cells of the placenta during pregnancy. It signals the corpus luteum to release progesterone, supporting pregnancy maintenance. Smaller amounts of hCG are also produced by the pituitary gland, liver, and colon.

Hypothalamic-pituitary-gonadal (HPG)- is a system of endocrine glands that regulates reproduction and associated behaviors in vertebrates. The HPG axis is made up of the hypothalamus, anterior pituitary gland, and gonads (ovaries or testes.

Ileum-the third portion of the small intestine.

Insulin resistance- happens when cells in your muscles, fat and liver don't respond as they should to insulin, a hormone your pancreas makes that's essential for life and regulating blood glucose (sugar) levels.

Leptin resistance- a condition where the body becomes less sensitive to leptin, a hormone that regulates appetite and energy use. This can lead to increased food intake and weight gain, even when there is enough or too much body fat.

Lipolysis-is a metabolic process that breaks down fat stores in the body to release energy. It's a vital process that occurs in most tissues and cell types, but is especially important when the body is fasting or exercising.

Mesolimbic pathways- a neural circuit in the brain that transmits dopamine from the ventral tegmental area (VTA) to the nucleus accumbens.

Neurofeedback- also known as EEG biofeedback, is a non-invasive brain-training technique that uses brain waves to help people change their brain activity and improve their health.

Oxytocin- a hormone that plays a role in many aspects of human life, including reproduction, behavior, and emotions.

Peptide YY-a hormone released by the gastrointestinal tract in response to eating that helps regulate appetite, gastric motility, and water and electrolyte absorption.

Progesterone- an endogenous steroid hormone that is commonly produced by the adrenal cortex as well as the gonads, which consist of the ovaries and the testes.

Serotonin- a chemical messenger that affects many bodily functions, including mood, sleep, digestion, and wound healing.

Serotonergic pathways- a system of neurons that use serotonin as a neurotransmitter to regulate a variety of functions in the brain and body.

Shatavari- also called Asparagus racemosus, is a root used in traditional Ayurvedic medicine. It is believed to boost female reproductive system.

Triphala-is a widely used herbal formulation in Indian traditional medicine that consists of fruits derived from three tree varieties.

Tyrosine- a nonessential amino acid the body makes from another amino acid called phenylalanine. It is an essential component for the production of several important brain chemicals called neurotransmitters, including epinephrine, norepinephrine, and dopamine.

Tryptophan- an essential amino acid that the body needs to function properly but cannot produce on its own. It's found in many foods, including meat, dairy, eggs, fish, nuts, seeds, and beans.

TSH-thyroid-stimulating hormone.

Ventral tegmental area (VTA)- is a midbrain structure that plays a role in a variety of behaviors and mental states,

- **Reward and Motivation:** The VTA houses dopamine neurons essential for reward processing, reinforcement, and emotional arousal.
- **Addiction and Depression:** Serving as a central hub, the VTA plays a significant role in addiction and depressive disorders.
- **Schizophrenia:** The VTA is associated with schizophrenia and other neuropsychiatric conditions.
- **Executive Function:** It also contributes to executive functions, such as decision-making and self-regulation.

Vertebrates- A vertebrate is an animal equipped with a backbone and a skeleton. Humans are vertebrates, along with many other animals. When you think of vertebrates, think of bones—these animals have a structured skeleton, particularly a backbone that safeguards their spinal cord.

Vertebrae- An irregularly shaped bone with a complex structure made of bone and some hyaline cartilage, the vertebra forms the vertebral column, or spine, in vertebrates. The proportions of each vertebra vary depending on its location within the spinal segments.

REFERENCES

The Link Between Hormones and Mental Health https://www.verywellmind.com/the-link-between-hormones-and-mental-health-7500077

Overview of the Endocrine System https://www.merckmanuals.com/professional/endocrine-and-metabolic-disorders/principles-of-endocrinology/overview-of-the-endocrine-system

10 Natural Ways to Balance Your Hormones https://www.healthline.com/nutrition/balance-hormones

Endocrine Disruptors https://www.niehs.nih.gov/health/topics/agents/endocrine

Estrogen: Hormone, Function, Levels & Imbalances https://my.clevelandclinic.org/health/body/22353-estrogen

Bigger, Faster, Stronger? 6 Benefits of Testosterone https://www.healthline.com/health/benefits-testosterone

How to Increase Progesterone Levels Naturally https://www.verywellhealth.com/natural-progesterone-8654810

The pros and cons of phytoestrogens - PMC - PubMed Central https://pmc.ncbi.nlm.nih.gov/articles/PMC3074428/

Role of Insulin in Health and Disease: An Update - PMC https://pmc.ncbi.nlm.nih.gov/articles/PMC8232639/

Insulin Resistance: Causes, symptoms, and prevention https://www.medicalnewstoday.com/articles/305567

Glucagon's Metabolic Action in Health and Disease - PMC https://www.ncbi.nlm.nih.gov/pmc/articles/PMC8513137/

Leptin, Obesity, and Leptin Resistance: Where Are We 25 ... https://pmc.ncbi.nlm.nih.gov/articles/PMC6893721/

How adrenaline can be a heart breaker https://www.bhf.org.uk/informationsupport/heart-matters-magazine/research/adrenaline

Cortisol Circadian Rhythm and its Impact on Health https://www.23nutritiontherapy.com/cortisol-circadian-rhythm/

Norepinephrine and Mental Health https://www.news-medical.net/health/Norepinephrine-and-Mental-Health.aspx

5 Impressive Herbs That Help Balance your Hormones https://www.healthline.com/nutrition/herbs-that-balance-hormones

Ghrelin: much more than a hunger hormone - PMC https://pmc.ncbi.nlm.nih.gov/articles/PMC4049314/

Factors affecting circulating levels of peptide YY in humans https://www.cambridge.org/core/journals/nutrition-research-reviews/article/factors-affecting-circulating-levels-of-peptide-yy-in-humans-a-comprehensive-review/61ECD6463880FEB7EEB72B60C9C065D2

Biochemistry, Cholecystokinin - StatPearls https://www.ncbi.nlm.nih.gov/books/NBK534204/

Ghrelin: What to know about the hunger hormone https://www.medicalnewstoday.com/articles/ghrelin-all-about-the-hunger-hormone

Thyroid Hormone Regulation of Metabolism https://journals.physiology.org/doi/abs/10.1152/physrev.00030.2013

Thyroid Disease: What It Is, Causes, Symptoms & Treatment https://my.clevelandclinic.org/health/diseases/8541-thyroid-disease

The Role of Nutrition on Thyroid Function - PMC - NCBI https://www.ncbi.nlm.nih.gov/pmc/articles/PMC11314468/#:

10 Ways to Boost Human Growth Hormone (HGH) Naturally https://www.healthline.com/nutrition/11-ways-to-increase-hgh

Melatonin: What It Is & Function - Cleveland Clinic https://my.clevelandclinic.org/health/articles/23411-melatonin

Exposure to Room Light before Bedtime Suppresses ... https://pmc.ncbi.nlm.nih.gov/articles/PMC3047226/

Cortisol Awakening Response - an overview https://www.sciencedirect.com/topics/neuroscience/cortisol-awakening-response

Natural Melatonin: 6 Ways to Increase Your Sleep Hormone https://www.goodrx.com/well-being/sleep/natural-melatonin

The Brain's Reward System in Health and Disease - PMC https://www.ncbi.nlm.nih.gov/pmc/articles/PMC8992377/

Physiology, Serotonin - StatPearls https://www.ncbi.nlm.nih.gov/books/NBK545168/

The role of oxytocin in social bonding, stress regulation ... https://www.sciencedirect.com/science/article/pii/S0306453013002369

10 Ways to Boost Dopamine and Serotonin Naturally https://www.goodtherapy.org/blog/10-ways-to-boost-dopamine-and-serotonin-naturally-1212177/

Physiology, Puberty - StatPearls https://www.ncbi.nlm.nih.gov/books/NBK534827/

Pregnancy Hormones' Impact on Emotional Health https://www.mindbodypregnancy.com/articles/pregnancy-hormones-impact-on-emotional-health

Male menopause: Myth or reality? https://www.mayoclinic.org/healthy-lifestyle/mens-health/in-depth/male-menopause/art-20048056

How to Balance Hormones Naturally https://www.verywellhealth.com/how-to-balance-hormones-naturally-8601400

How Does Food Affect Your Hormones? https://www.mariongluckclinic.com/blog/how-does-food-affect-your-hormones.html

The Top 5 Hormone Balancing Superfoods https://nourishmedicine.com/top-5-super foods-hormonal-balance/

How Sugar Causes Hormonal Imbalance https://www.womenshealthnetwork.com/hormonal-imbalance/hormonal-imbalance-caused-by-sugar/

10 Natural Ways to Balance Your Hormones https://www.healthline.com/nutrition/balance-hormones

8 Ayurvedic Practices For Hormonal Harmony https://www.ayurvedainstitute.co.uk/finding-the-perfect-balance-8-ayurvedic-practices-for-hormonal-harmony/

Balancing Hormones with Traditional Chinese Medicine https://www.totalwellnesscen tre.ca/resources/2024/4/2/balancing-hormones-with-traditional-chinese-medi cine

Integrating Eastern and Western Medicine - ThatGYNDoctor https://www.thatgyndoc tor.com/post/integrating-eastern-and-western-medicine-enhancing-women-s-health

Ayurveda and Traditional Chinese Medicine https://pmc.ncbi.nlm.nih.gov/arti cles/PMC1297513/

12 Adaptogens to Balance, Restore and Protect the Body https://draxe.com/nutrition/adaptogenic-herbs-adaptogens/

Yoga Sequence for a Hormonal Imbalance https://www.yogajournal.com/lifestyle/health/womens-health/yoga-sequence-hormonal-imbalance/

Endocrine-Disrupting Chemicals (EDCs) https://www.endocrine.org/patient-engage ment/endocrine-library/edcs

Hormones and Social Connection: The Surprising Link ... https://tnthealthyhormones. com/hormones-and-social-connection-the-surprising-link-between-relation ships-and-hormonal-health/

5 common myths about hormone imbalances https://www.mdanderson.org/cancer wise/5-common-myths-about-hormone imbalances-and-thyroid-function.h00-159538956.html

Lifestyle Factors and Hormone Levels https://www.bodylogicmd.com/blog/lifestyle-factors-and-hormone-levels/

Bioidentical Hormones: Therapy, Uses, Safety & Side Effects https://my.clevelandclinic. org/health/treatments/15660-bioidentical-hormones

Natural hormone replacements: Benefits and side effects https://www.medicalnewstoday. com/articles/natural-hormone-replacements

Mindfulness & Its Benefits For Your Hormones https://drjenhardie.com/blog/post/mindfulness-its-benefits-for-your-hormones

10 apps to help you embrace self-care https://www.cnet.com/tech/services-and-soft ware/10-apps-to-help-you-embrace-self-care/

Circadian Rhythms and Hormonal Homeostasis https://www.ncbi.nlm.nih.gov/pmc/articles/PMC5372003/

5 Impressive Herbs That Help Balance your Hormones https://www.healthline.com/nutrition/herbs-that-balance-hormones

Natural treatments for PCOS: Evidence-based methods https://www.medicalnewstoday.com/articles/326560

Thyroid Disease: What It Is, Causes, Symptoms & Treatment https://my.clevelandclinic.org/health/diseases/8541-thyroid-disease

Adrenal fatigue does not exist: a systematic review - PMC https://www.ncbi.nlm.nih.gov/pmc/articles/PMC4997656/

10 Natural Ways to Balance Your Hormones https://www.healthline.com/nutrition/balance-hormones

Hormones, HRT and advocating for yourself https://www.balance-menopause.com/menopause-library/hormones-hrt-and-advocating-for-yourself/

15 Questions to Ask Your Hormone Doctor About HRT https://www.bodylogicmd.com/blog/15-questions-to-ask-your-hormone-doctor-about-hrt/

Hormona: Home https://www.hormona.io/

Hormone Testing 101: How to Test and Interpret Your Results https://www.rupahealth.com/post/hormone-testing-101-how-to-test-and-interpret-your-results

2023 in Review: Advancements in Hormone Replacement ... https://www.sottopelletherapy.com/blog/2023-in-review-advancements-in-physician-hormone-replacement-therapy-training/

Precision Medicine for Endocrinology - PMC https://www.ncbi.nlm.nih.gov/pmc/articles/PMC5219894/

Wearable Patch Wirelessly Monitors Estrogen in Sweat https://www.caltech.edu/about/news/wearable-patch-wirelessly-monitors-estrogen-in-sweat

Genome Editing Applications of CRISPR/Cas9 in Metabolic ... https://www.frontiersin.org/research-topics/44932/genome-editing-applications-of-crisprcas9-in-metabolic-diseases-hormonal-system-and-cancer-research/magazine

Cadman, B. (2023, July 19). *What are the health benefits of shatavari?* https://www.medicalnewstoday.com/articles/322043

New Approach to Diagnosing and Staging Diabetes Developed Using Optoacoustic and Machine Learning Techniques - Khalifa University. https://www.ku.ac.ae/new-approach-to-diagnosing-and-staging-diabetes-developed-using-optoacoustic-and-machine-learning-techniques

Can Endometriosis Be Cured? | Honjok.ME. https://honjok.me/diseases/can-cure-endometriosis/

Endometriosis - Clinicpark. https://clinicpark.com/endometriosis/

Ovarian cyst treatment options in Delhi - Party.biz. http://mail.party.biz/forums/topic/233218/ovarian-cyst-treatment-options-in-delhi